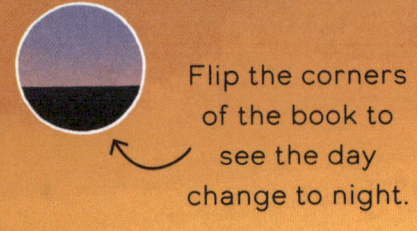
Flip the corners of the book to see the day change to night.

For the human and non-human mammals in my family – L.N.
For my niece and nephew, My and Huy – X.L.

A TEMPLAR BOOK

First published in the UK in 2023 by Templar Books,
an imprint of Bonnier Books UK
4th Floor, Victoria House,
Bloomsbury Square, London WC1B 4DA
Owned by Bonnier Books
Sveavägen 56, Stockholm, Sweden
www.bonnierbooks.co.uk

Text copyright © 2023 by Lela Nargi
Illustration copyright © 2023 by Xuan Le
Design copyright © 2023 by Templar Books

1 3 5 7 9 10 8 6 4 2

All rights reserved

ISBN 978-1-78741-934-6

Edited by Carly Blake
Designed by Jeni Child
Production by Neil Randles

Printed in China

Wherever you see this icon,
recharge the page under a lamp while you read.
Then turn off the lights to see what glows!

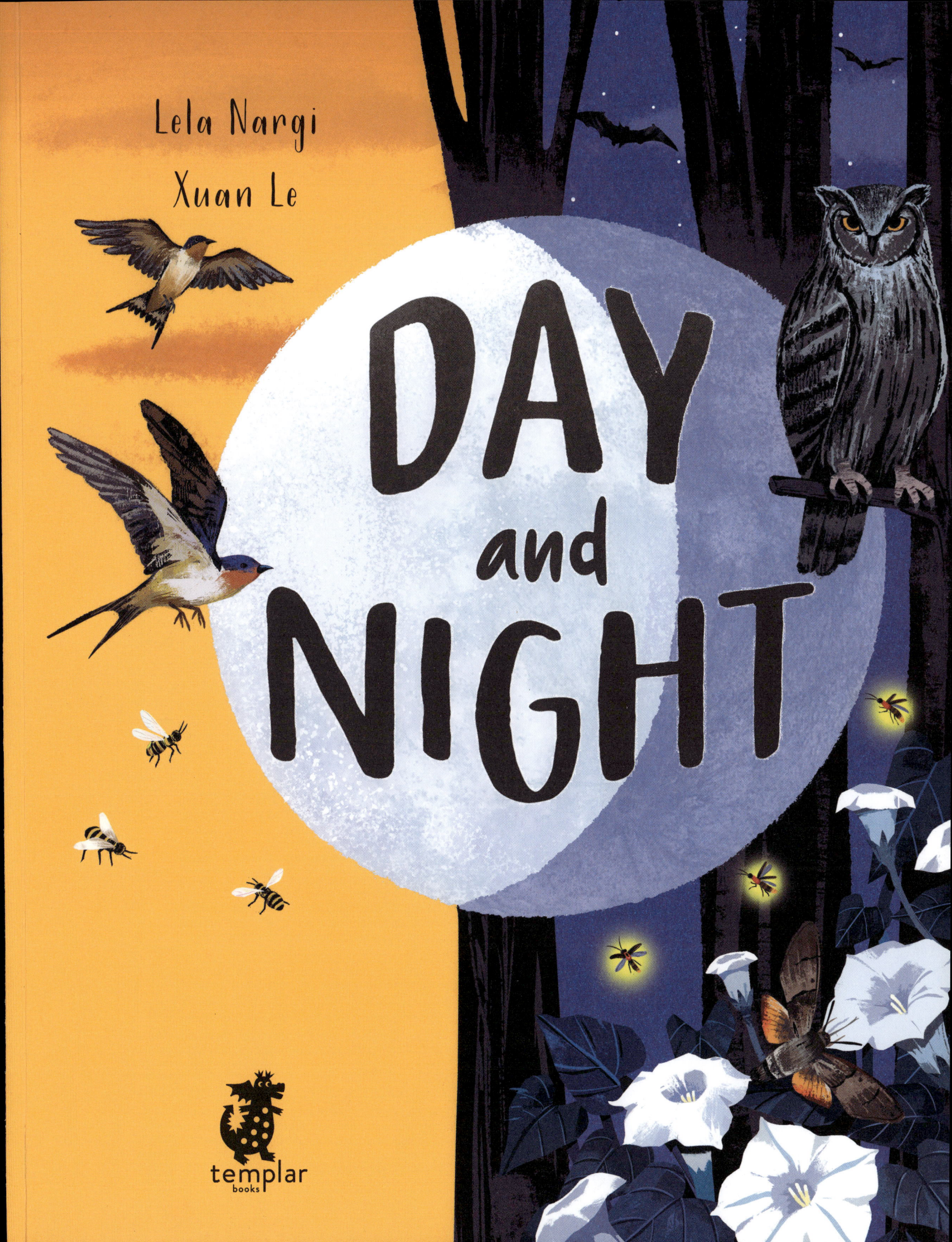

The velvety night feels like it will linger forever.
But all at once there's a shift.

You might think a mule deer's enormous ears would help it hear **PREDATORS**. But it's their amazing eyesight in low light and keen sense of smell that help them to sense a big cat **STALKING** nearby.

Mule deer are **HERBIVORES**. They eat plants, such as dandelion, clover and sagebrush.

Deer can see shades of blue best, which is ideal in the inky twilight.

The deep dark pales, giving way to the day's first light.
The quiet flutters as birds call to one another.

Here in Western North America, mule deer nibble at leaves while a mountain lion watches.

Mountain lions are CARNIVORES. They eat meat.

So it happens that the world of shadows tiptoes towards day.

Often hidden in the dim light, mountain lions hunt bighorn sheep, porcupines, turkeys and even insects. One mule deer, though, can feed a mountain lion for a week.

The sun rises like a hush. It reaches out its rays, brushing away the last patches of night, as it inches over the horizon.

In Western Australia, spiderwebs glitter with last night's dew.

After spinning webs in the evening to catch insect **PREY**, orb weaver spiders take them down in the morning by eating the silk.

Morning dew caught in the webs quenches the spiders' thirst.

Why does the sun look red at sunrise? When the sun is low in the sky, its light travels through a thicker layer of **ATMOSPHERE** to reach us. On this long journey, some of the light is scattered away but the reds and yellows make it to us.

But orb weaver spiders busily take them down. They must find a place to hide as hungry honey eaters dart from their nests.

The New Holland honey eater not only eats spiders, but also uses spider silk to hold its grass-and-leaf nests together.

Another of the honey eater's favourite foods is flower nectar, which it harvests in the early morning, before bees come out to forage for nectar, too.

Little by little, the morning light deepens to gold.
Here in the north of Mexico, more of the world awakens.

Mexican sunflowers bask in the sun.
They offer their pollen to hairy little bees
beginning their low-pitched buzz.

Many bees visit flowers throughout the day. But some **POLLINATORS**, like sunflower bees, are active in the early morning.

Sunflower bees are solitary. They live alone in nests they make in the ground. Once the bees are warm enough, they leave their nests for the day.

Mexican sunflowers aren't true sunflowers, which can turn their heads to follow the sun. But they, too, love the rays, which warm their petals for visiting bees. Their yellow colour is a bee favourite.

Hummingbirds zip up to tube-shaped flowers for a long drink.

Like bees, hummingbirds are pollinators. They carry pollen from flower to flower, which helps to make more plants. When a hummingbird visits a flower, it unfurls its long tongue, which it keeps coiled inside its head.

The brightening sun climbs in the sky.

Under its light, a pack of African wild dogs rest and clean each other. Their bellies are full after a dawn hunt.

As a pet, a dog lives with its humans, keeping them company in the day and sleeping when they sleep at night. In the wild, African wild dogs live in packs and hunt in the morning, before it gets too hot to move, or at the end of the day.

Pigeons strut and murmur. They nibble at fruit on trees.

The African green pigeon eats mainly fruit, such as figs. It might hang upside down from a branch to reach them. Although they have sensitive eyesight, pigeons see best and clearest in daytime.

Pigeons live almost everywhere in the world, including here in South Africa. Though these smart birds famously thrive in cities, around 300 pigeon species live in the true wild, where there are no crumbs left by humans for them to scavenge.

Over the Andes Mountains in South America, the late morning sun blazes like a spotlight.

Andean condors are the largest flying land birds in the Americas. Their 3-metre wingspans make them look like scary predators. But condors are **SCAVENGERS** — they feed on the flesh of dead animals, known as **CARRION**. Their eating habits stop diseases from spreading and help keep **ECOSYSTEMS** healthy.

Condors soar on warm air currents. Their wide wings darken the ground as they circle, scouting for a meal.

As the day heats up, warm air rises and creates currents, which these enormous, heavy birds ride on.

Guanacos graze on plants such as grasses and herbs during the day.

These woolly animals have excellent hearing and smell to help them detect danger nearby. However, their poor eyesight means they might not see a predator until it's too late.

The sun rises higher until it is straight overhead and all shadows are swallowed up by the light.

In the tropical jungles of Malaysia emperor cicadas rattle and hiss from tree trunks.

Even on very hot summer days in this jungle, emperor cicadas chirrup loudly. This sound comes from a muscle in their abdomens called a **TYMBAL**. A cicada twitches its tymbals to make its ribs SNAP apart — up to around 400 times a second!

Cicada males make noise to attract females. The hotter it is, the more friction they can make in their bodies, and the louder they become.

Nearby, a chameleon forest dragon stretches on a branch.

Chameleon forest dragons are not actually chameleons but they can still change colours. This helps them blend in with their daytime surroundings and avoid predators.

These reptiles spend their days in trees, hunting for cicadas and other insects.

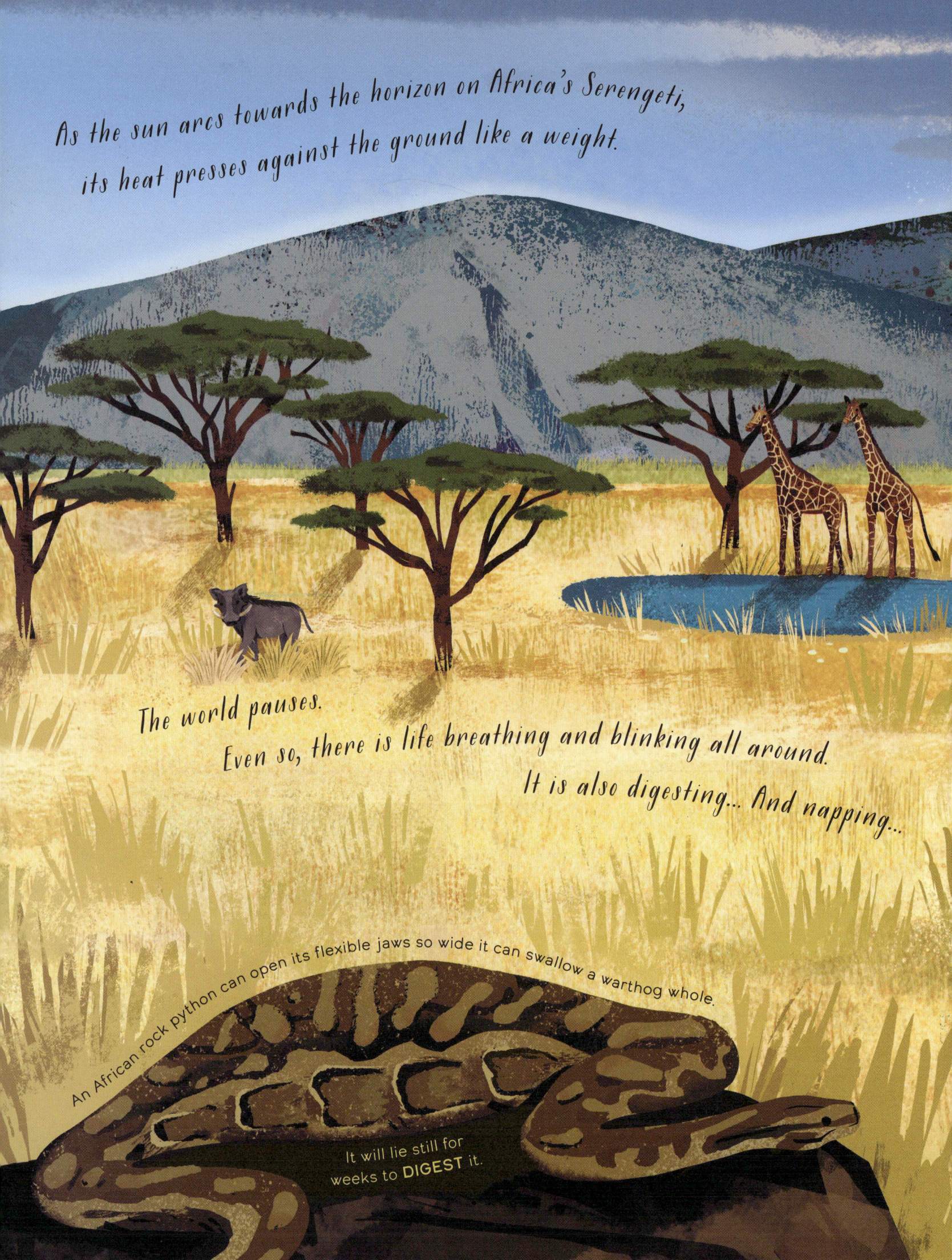

As the sun arcs towards the horizon on Africa's Serengeti, its heat presses against the ground like a weight.

The world pauses.
Even so, there is life breathing and blinking all around.
It is also digesting... And napping...

An African rock python can open its flexible jaws so wide it can swallow a warthog whole.

It will lie still for weeks to DIGEST it.

On the African **SAVANNA**, summertime is rainy season. Days may start out sunny, but as hot, humid air rises to meet cooler air, rain comes, and it may fall for hours. African elephants can hear rain falling more than 200 kilometres away. They love to splash and play in it, but sometimes they prefer to take shelter and stay dry!

And taking shelter from an afternoon rain shower.

Like most cats, the caracal is usually active at night. But it has also adapted to hunting in the daytime, when there is more food on offer. Its sand-coloured fur acts as **CAMOUFLAGE**.

A caracal can leap 3 metres into the air to snatch bird prey, such as crested guinea fowl.

Some creatures have been on the move all day.

European swallows **MIGRATE** nearly 10,000 kilometres between Europe and Southern Africa twice a year.

Before they fly, swallows fuel up on big, juicy insects, such as horseflies. Then, when the afternoon is warm and the winds are calm, they start their long journey.

Swallows can fly up to 300 kilometres a day, on routes that may take them over the Sahara Desert.

Even now, as the sun begins to fall and the sky turns pink, swallows swoop tirelessly over a river in the north of Europe.

Tiny caddisflies are furry-winged, moth-like bugs. Females swarm to lay their eggs in rivers and streams by day and into the evening. Larvae hatch, then weave together pebbles, twigs and leaves. They **PUPATE** inside these clever homes, then emerge weeks later as adult caddisflies.

The sun sinks and the sky flares red over Fiji as evening sighs in. Daytime dwellers seek out resting spots for the night...

During the day on the coral reef, colourful plant-eating fish feed on nutritious seagrass and seaweed. These plants soak up vitamins while the sun shines.

As day turns to night on the reef, daytime fish tuck themselves into their holes to sleep and nighttime fish slowly begin to emerge.

And new faces peek out from their sleeping holes, ready for 'breakfast'!

Corals begin to wake up as the light fades. They feed at night.

Did you know that coral is alive? A reef is made of colonies of tiny creatures that are related to jellyfish and sea anemones. They are called coral **POLYPS**. They open at night to feed on the tiny animals and plants known as **PLANKTON**.

As the fading sun drops behind the horizon, edges melt into each other in the low light.

Here in North America, little brown bats stream from their roosts in the cliffs. They circle in the air, gobbling insects as they go.

One little brown bat can eat 1,000 mosquitoes, beetles and moths in an hour. The bats make sounds that bounce off the flying insects. This is called **ECHOLOCATION** and it helps the bats find the insects in the dark. They hunt at night to avoid competing with other insect-eaters, like birds.

There's a flash.
Then a hundred more.

Fireflies pulse green
among the leaves.

Bats are not so keen on fireflies. That's because they taste terrible!

A firefly's glow warns predators not to eat it.
It also signals to potential mates to say, "Here I am!". Nighttime is the best time to see those flickering messages.

Darkness creeps in until all memory of day is erased.

Moonflowers, also called evening glories, open as soon as night falls. They release a smell that attracts night **POLLINATORS**, such as moths. The white petals of the moonflower glow in moonlight to give these insects extra help in finding them.

In South Asia, snow-white moonflowers open wide.
Moths flicker through the cool air,
lured by the sweet smell of nectar and the glow of petals.

The hawkmoth has a long, tube-like tongue, called a **PROBOSCIS**. It is long enough to reach the nectar deep inside a moonflower. A hawkmoth can hover in the air while it feeds. Some moths come out in the day or the evening. But nocturnal moths have evolved to navigate using the moon and stars.

Shhh! In this Canadian forest the trees are sleeping! They slowly let their branches droop in the darkness.

A mushroom is a fungus's above-ground part, which may pop up overnight when the air is cool and damp. It contains **SPORES**. A fungus's underground part is made up of root-like **MYCELIUM**.

Trees really do 'sleep' at night. As the sun goes down, they slowly, slowly relax their branches. Scientists have recorded trees drooping by as much as 10 centimetres. Their branches begin to rise again at dawn as the trees wake up.

Mushrooms glow on dead tree trunks and in the dirt between live tree roots. Ants and beetles come to nibble them.

Mushrooms are not plants, which all belong to the plant **KINGDOM**. They belong to their own group of organisms – the fungus kingdom.

Some fungi are **BIOLUMINESCENT**. That means they can make their own light. This attracts insects, such as ants. Ants eat the spores, then poop them out as they scuttle through the forest. This makes more fungi.

A nighttime breeze pushes through the trees by an English river. It tickles awake an otter napping on the bank.

Otters have excellent eyesight, which helps them spot prey. They also have sensitive whiskers, which let them sense eels and other fish moving nearby.

In the evening and at night, otters dive into the water — as deep as 18 metres — to capture prey. They can close their ears and noses so water can't get in.

It has been dreaming of dinner, of the tasty eels sneaking along the muddy riverbed.

Eels are very shy and secretive animals. Freshwater eels spend their days buried in mud on riverbeds. At night they feed on other fish and molluscs, such as snails.

European eels are born in seagrass forests in the Sargasso Sea near Bermuda. They drift as eggs on an epic journey across the ocean for up to 10,000 kilometres, growing and changing over several years. Eventually they find their way up rivers.

When they are 20 or more years old, they return to the Sargasso Sea to breed. Then they die.

At the north and south of the planet, colourful lights steal the sky from the stars.

In the Northern Hemisphere, these lights are called the Northern Lights or the aurora borealis.

This phenomenon, called aurora, is caused by solar storms.

Solar storms on the surface of the sun shoot out charged particles. When they reach our **ATMOSPHERE**, some get trapped in Earth's magnetic field and travel to the poles. There the particles mix with oxygen and nitrogen to give us colourful light shows.

Dovekies are Arctic birds that spend their lives on and around the ice. They feed both day and night, diving 30 metres into the water to catch crustaceans and other food.

Walruses can sleep anywhere! Scientists have discovered that they can snooze as they float on top of the water, lying at the bottom of it, or standing and leaning against an object (or friend!) on land.

They glow red and purple and green, swirling in every direction.

The Southern Hemisphere has the Southern Lights or aurora australis. They can be seen near the South Pole.

Antarctic fur seals feed at night. Their favourite prey are lanternfish and squid.

Penguins never take a deep slumber, preferring to nap instead. This keeps them alert to the seals that want to eat them.

On the East Coast of the United States, late night bustles with songbirds following stars across the black sky. They soar high over forests, and far out over the ocean.

Some songbirds migrate thousands of kilometres in spring and autumn, to and from the places they were born. They travel by night, when there are fewer predators awake for them to worry about. Earth's magnetic pull helps guide the birds. They also use the stars to find their way. Scientists believe baby birds in their nests learn to read **CONSTELLATIONS** as if they were maps.

They see the moon as it's swallowed by clouds.
They see tiny spots glittering on wave tops.

Bioluminescence not only lights up fireflies and mushrooms, it makes the sea sparkle too.
Tiny organisms light up in the water when waves wash over them.

The bright light of the moon catches rippling waves off an island in the Indian Ocean.

Giant coconut crabs come out of their **BURROWS** in the dark, when the air is cool and there is less danger of them drying out. These 2-kilogram crabs are **CANNIBALS**. That means they eat their own kind. They also eat fallen coconuts, which they crack open with their powerful pincers. They can even climb trees to hunt birds, such as the red-footed booby.

It glistens off the shiny shells of crabs on the shore.
It shimmers across satiny feathers.

Unlike songbirds, many seabirds migrate during the day. The red-footed booby, though, stays put all year long. It does travel — but only out to sea to hunt for fish.

At night red-footed boobies **ROOST** in trees off the ground. They tuck their heads under their back feathers to keep warm.

As the darkness begins to fade away in this Japanese forest, dim light catches the surface of a river. Even in the dark an owl can spot its dinner.

Owls have a special layer at the back of their eyes that reflects light. This give owls super night vision. It also makes an owl's eyes appear to glow, which is called **EYESHINE**.

Unlike many other owls, the Blakiston's fish owl spends a lot of its hunting time on the ground near rivers. Its favourite meal is fish. Although it usually hunts as night begins to fall, it may hunt all night long when it is rearing chicks.

The Blakiston's fish owl is the largest owl in the world, and it is **ENDANGERED**.

Like other species of pike (also known as pickerel), the Amur pike is a freshwater fish with very sharp teeth!

Silently it pounces and pulls out a giant fish from the water.

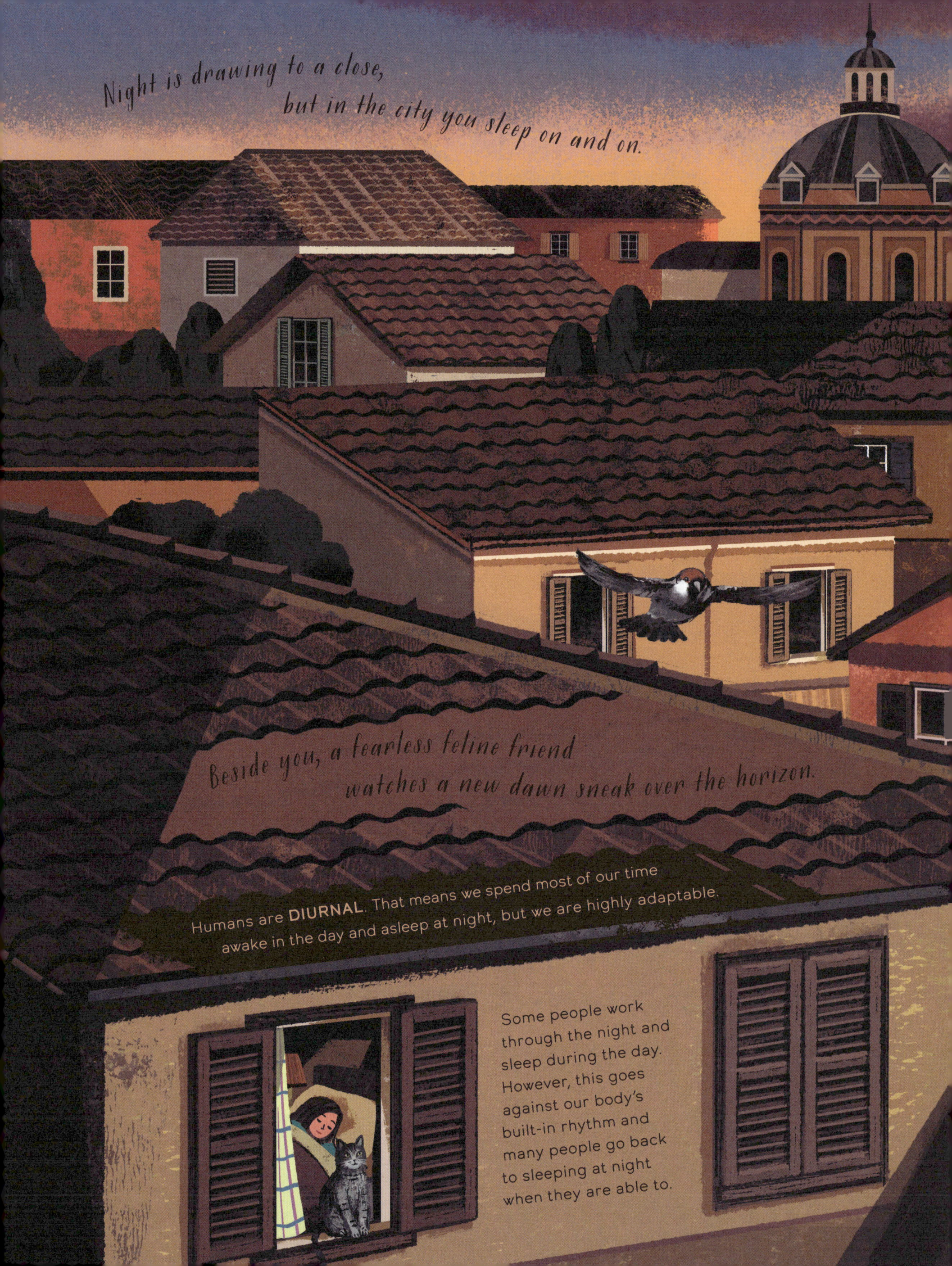

Night is drawing to a close, but in the city you sleep on and on.

Beside you, a fearless feline friend watches a new dawn sneak over the horizon.

Humans are **DIURNAL**. That means we spend most of our time awake in the day and asleep at night, but we are highly adaptable.

Some people work through the night and sleep during the day. However, this goes against our body's built-in rhythm and many people go back to sleeping at night when they are able to.

The sky begins to brighten once more as the chirp and chatter of a new day begins.

Housecats are adaptable, too. They are nocturnal, hunting at night and sleeping during the day. However, when they live with people, they often adjust to our schedules, staying awake for parts of the day to get strokes and treats.

A Guide to Day and Night

Dawn

Before the sun has risen above the horizon, the sky lightens. This time of day is also known as twilight.

Animals and plants that are active in twilight are called **CREPUSCULAR**.

Sunrise

The sun rises higher, eventually coming up over the horizon line, warming the air.

Daytime

The period between sunrise and sunset, when the sun peeks up over the horizon line then travels in an arc across the sky. It is warmer than it is at night and there is more food around, but animals are more easily spotted by predators in the light.

Animals and plants that are active in daytime are called **DIURNAL**.

Polar night and midnight sun

At the very north and south of Earth, days work differently. For six months of the year the sun never rises above the horizon. This is called the **POLAR NIGHT**, and it is dark all the time. For the other six months of the year, the sun never falls below the horizon. This is called the **MIDNIGHT SUN**, and it is light all the time.

This phenomenon happens because Earth is tilted. When one pole is tilted towards the sun, the other pole is tilted away. This makes daytime or nighttime last more than 24 hours in these places.

Sunset

The sun sinks below the horizon line, causing light and warmth to fade.

DIURNAL animals and plants prepare to rest for the night.

Dusk

The sun lowers even more, even though we can't see it now. The sky grows darker but there is still a faint glow of light. This time of day is also known as twilight.

CREPUSCULAR animals and plants are active again.

Night

The period between dusk and dawn, when it is dark. The air is cool and more humid. There is less food around at night but under the cover of darkness animals can avoid getting caught by predators.

Animals that are active at night are called **NOCTURNAL**.

GLOSSARY

Words shown in **CAPITAL LETTERS** in the book are explained here.

ATMOSPHERE: The layer of gasses that surrounds Earth.

BIOLUMINESCENT: Animals or other organisms that can make their own light are bioluminescent.

BURROW: A shelter dug in the ground by an animal.

CAMOUFLAGE: Colour, shape or pattern that makes an animal hard to see in its surroundings.

CANNIBAL: An animal that eats its own kind.

CARNIVORE: An animal that eats other animals.

CARRION: The flesh of a dead animal. Scavengers such as condors eat carrion.

CONSTELLATION: A group of stars in the sky that humans may see as forming the shape of an animal, such as a swan, or an object, such as a plough.

DIGEST: The process by which our bodies break down food so that we can use it for energy.

ECHOLOCATION: The way animals, such as bats, find objects in the dark using sound.

ECOSYSTEM: The plants, animals and other organisms that live in an environment and interact with each other to survive.

ENDANGERED: At risk of dying out.

EYESHINE: Light reflected in an animal's eye at night, which lets it see extremely well in the dark.

HERBIVORE: An animal that eats only plants.

HORIZON: The place where Earth meets sky.

KINGDOM: All living things are organised into groups that help us identify them. The biggest of these groups are called kingdoms and there are five of them: Animal, Plant, Fungi, Protist and Monera.

MIGRATION: The movement of animals with the seasons, to find enough food to eat and to stay warm or cool.

MYCELIUM: The biggest part of a fungus, which is made up of a network of tiny threads called hyphae. The mycelium usually lives underground, but also in places such as decaying tree trunks.

PLANKTON: Tiny plants, animals and other marine organisms. Plankton is the main source of food for many ocean creatures.

POLLINATOR: An animal that helps plants reproduce by moving pollen from one flower to another.

POLYP: A tiny sea creature. Colonies of polyps make up the living part of coral.

PREDATOR: An animal that hunts and eats other animals as its prey (see below).

PREY: An animal that is hunted by other animals, known as predators (see above).

PROBOSCIS: A long tube-like mouthpart. Hummingbirds and butterflies use theirs to drink nectar from flowers. An elephant's trunk is also called a proboscis and is used for many activities, including drinking and spouting water.

PUPATE: The stage when an insect larva, such as a butterfly caterpillar, turns into a form called a pupa. This happens inside a protective case and the insect is inactive during this time. A butterfly's pupa case is called a chrysalis. Inside the chrysalis, the pupa turns into a new butterfly and then emerges.

ROOST: To settle down to sleep. Many birds roost at night.

SAVANNA: A habitat, also known as tropical grassland, that can be found in the regions just above and below the equator. It is covered with many types of grasses and a scattering of trees and shrubs.

SCAVENGER: An animal that eats animals that are already dead.

SPORE: The tiny, seed-like part of a fungus.

STALK: To hunt stealthily, like a predatory cat hunting bird prey.

TYMBAL: A cicada has a hard shell covering the outside of its body, called an exoskeleton. The tymbal is the part of the exoskeleton it vibrates to make sound.

Gasholders

A History in Pictures

Edited by National Grid plc,
Russell Thomas and Timur Tatlioglu

Published by Liverpool University Press on behalf of Historic England, The Engine House, Fire Fly Avenue, Swindon SN2 2EH
www.HistoricEngland.org.uk

Historic England is a Government service championing England's heritage and giving expert, constructive advice.

© 2024 National Grid plc

nationalgrid

The views contained in this book are those of the authors alone and not Historic England or Liverpool University Press.

First published 2024

ISBN: 978-1-83553-849-4

British Library Cataloguing in Publication data
A CIP catalogue record for this book is available from the British Library.

National Grid plc have asserted the right to be identified as the editors of this book in accordance with the Copyright, Designs and Patents Act 1988.

All rights reserved
No part of this publication may be reproduced or transmitted in any form or by any means, electronic or mechanical, including photocopying, recording, or any information storage or retrieval system, without permission in writing from the publisher.

Application for the reproduction of images should be made to Historic England Archive. Every effort has been made to trace the copyright holders and we apologise in advance for any unintentional omissions, which we would be pleased to correct in any subsequent edition of this book.

Typeset in Charter 9/11

Page layout by Carnegie Book Production

Printed in the Czech Republic via Akcent Media Limited

Front cover: Kennington, London, c 1950. The Oval Cricket Ground with the No 1 gasholder visible behind. [© NGA]
Back cover: Bethnal Green, London. [© St William]

Contents

Foreword — vii

Preface — viii

Contributors — viii

Acknowledgements — ix

Abbreviations — ix

1	Introduction	1
2	Evolution of gasholders	15
3	Column-guided gasholders	35
4	Frame-guided gasholders	56
5	Spiral-guided gasholders	79
6	Waterless gasholders	98
7	High-pressure gasholders	111
8	Gasholder construction	128
9	Gasholders on the landscape	144
10	Gasholders and society	165
11	Gasholder engineers and manufacturers	187
12	The future	206

Further resources — 226

References — 226

Index — 227

Foreword

Gasholders, for nearly two centuries, were a familiar, striking and often beloved element of almost every city-, town- and villagescape in England. Since 2010 the technological advancements that gave rise to the structures have rendered them obsolete. Gas fuelled the first streetlamps and illuminated our homes and places of work, and the specialised technology required to achieve those feats was so advanced that it was exported across the world.

A unique hybrid structure – part building and part machine – the gasholder evolved from the small counterweighted examples of the 1820s to the towering cylindrical frames which loomed large over the communities they served. The 1960s change from carbonised coal gas to imported natural gas saw many of the 19th- and 20th-century town gasworks demolished, although the gasholders which served them continued in use, and at the start of the 21st century there were more than 600 functioning examples across the United Kingdom.

From the late 20th century there was a transition away from gasholders as below-ground high-pressure pipes were introduced, a more cost-effective and scalable gas storage technique. Since 2010, National Grid, the owner of the majority of gasholders in the United Kingdom, has been engaged in a programme of decommissioning, decontaminating and dismantling of its gasholder portfolio, working closely with Historic England to capture a final and detailed record. This substantial body of information records the technological innovation, design variety and significance of gasholders which enabled such a transformation in both domestic and industrial life.

This book, produced and funded by National Grid and authored by an international authority on the history of the gas industry along with the collaboration of Historic England, details the history of gasholder development from the early designs of pioneering engineer Samuel Clegg, to their final redundancy and dismantling. Throughout, the dominant place of gasholders on the skyline and in our communities is captured through historic and contemporary photography, which charts how the gasholders remained as the landscapes around them evolved.

Though they are much diminished in number and remain an exceptionally challenging structure to preserve and repurpose, gasholders retain a special place within the public consciousness, and this book, filled with striking images of their gas bells gracefully ascending the frames, is a fitting record of their contribution to the making of modern Britain.

Phil Edwards
Head of Commercial Property,
National Grid plc

Preface

This book is a photographic record of gasholders and the gasworks sites on which they were found. It is dedicated to all those who have been involved in the design, construction, operation, maintenance, dismantling, preservation and reuse of gasholders and the regeneration of gasworks over their many years of existence. It is not intended as a detailed history but provides a short written historical context to the photographs provided.

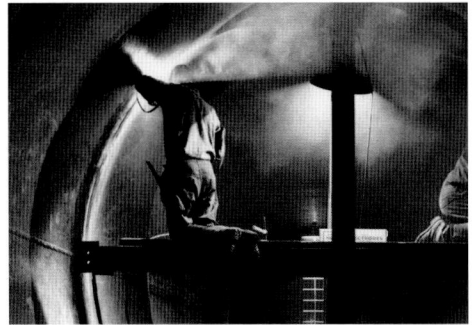

Contributors

This book has been produced and edited by Nadia Dew, Philippa Meares, Phil Edwards and Chris Taylor of National Grid plc. The photographs were collated and curated by Russell Thomas with the input of the other contributors. The written commentary was provided by Russell Thomas of WSP (Chapters 1–11) and Timur Tatlioglu of Montagu Evans (Chapter 12). Matthew Bristow and Shane Gould from Historic England have also been actively involved in its production.

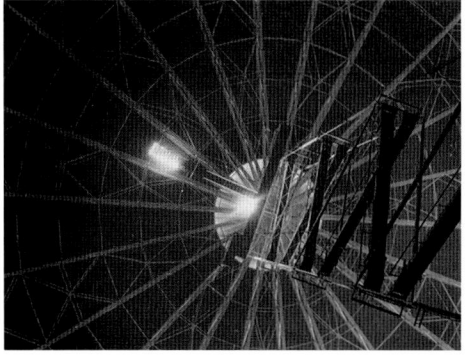

Acknowledgements

This book was only possible due to the dedication of those who have taken the time to record and preserve the history of the gas industry. It was edited and sponsored by National Grid plc, and authored by Russell Thomas (Chapters 1–11), and Timur Tatliogu (Chapter 12).

Others who have made significant contributions include National Grid's supply chain, the IGEM History Panel, John Horne, Brian Sturt and the late Barry Wilkinson in particular, and the staff and volunteers named who have provided their images for use in this book, from the National Gas Archive, National Gas Museum and St William (part of the Berkeley Group). We also acknowledge Historic England, whose photographers have diligently recorded the sites from the ground and air, in particular Chris Redgrave, Damian Grady, Anna Bridson and James Davies.

Abbreviations

GLCC	Gas Light and Coke Company
IGEM	Institution of Gas Engineers and Managers History Panel Archive
LGM	Leicester Gas Museum
LNG	Liquefied Natural Gas
LPG	Liquefied Petroleum Gas
NGA	National Gas Archive
RSJ	Rolled Steel Joist
ft	Feet

Fig 1.1
Portrait of William Murdoch, 1823, by John Graham-Gilbert.
[© Birmingham Museums Trust]

1 Introduction

This book is dedicated to gasholders and those who have worked with them, structures which have been part of our industrial heritage since the first decade of the 19th century. They were found on gasworks, sites which manufactured gas from fossil fuels such as coal and oil. Gasworks had a profound impact on the landscape from their striking visual appearance, but also culturally, socially and environmentally, through the people they served and employed and the environmental legacy they left behind.

It was the Scottish engineer William Murdoch (Fig 1.1) who undertook the work to develop a commercial process for lighting factories with gas, while working for the steam engine manufacturer Boulton and Watt at their Soho Foundry in Smethwick, West Midlands. Murdoch's experiments led to this being the first industrial building in the world to be lit by gas.

While perfecting the process, Murdoch's apprentice, Samuel Clegg, had grown tired of the delays and set up as a rival gas engineer. It was Clegg who in 1805 first lit Henry Lodge's Willow Hall Mill in Sowerby Bridge, Yorkshire, a few weeks before Murdoch lit the Salford Twist Mill of Philips and Lee.

Gasworks were then constructed at mills and factories across the country. Some of these gasworks then grew beyond their own needs and became a gasworks supplying other factories and the local community (Fig 1.2).

The first gas company to provide a public gas supply was formed during the reign of King George III. It was promoted for many years by the German entrepreneur Friedrich Winzer who had lit Pall Mall with gas in 1807. It features in the background of his portrait (Fig 1.3).

The Gas Light and Coke Company (GLCC) was established in 1812 and built its first gasworks on Great Peter Street in Westminster, London. They supplied Westminster, London and parts of Southwark. Soon many other rival gas companies were established, first in London, then across the United Kingdom and eventually around the world. The gas was burnt to provide gas lighting to streets (Fig 1.4), public buildings and those wealthy enough to light their homes.

The GLCC went on to build the largest gasworks in the world at Beckton on the northern bank of the River Thames (Fig 1.5).

The manufacture of gas from coal involved heating the coal in cylindrical vessels called retorts, which can be seen in Fig 1.6.

As the coal was heated it would decompose, releasing the gas and other impurities. The impurities had to be removed to make the gas safe to use as shown in Fig 1.7. This involved cooling the gas using condensers to remove tar, washing the gas in washers and scrubbers, and purifying the gas of harmful sulphur and cyanide. The cleaned gas was stored in gasholders, ready for distribution to customers.

The types of plant used to remove impurities from the gas can be seen in Figs 1.8 and 1.9.

Whereas the Beckton gasworks were built on a massive scale, most gasworks were quite small, supplying towns and large villages. The entire staff of the Alresford gasworks, with a single-lift gasholder behind, can be seen in Fig 1.10.

The gasworks at Blakeney (Fig 1.11) in Gloucestershire were even smaller, and so was the plant required to clean the gas.

The gasworks at Sherbourne (Fig 1.12) were more typical of the size of most town gasworks in the United Kingdom and like those that survive at the Fakenham Gas Museum (Fig 1.13).

The gasholder was a key piece of equipment, as gas use fluctuated throughout the day and night. It acted as a buffer between gas production and supply, storing supply at times of low demand and releasing it at times of high demand. The operation of a gasholder is shown in Fig 1.14.

Gasworks required good transport links such as a canal, river or railway to import coal and export by-products. They also needed access to a plentiful supply of water for use in gasworks processes. Bath gasworks (Fig 1.15) had transport connection by rail and river. Being close to rivers, gasworks were susceptible to flooding as seen in the case of Windsor (Fig 1.16). Some larger gasworks had their own locomotives to move the coal around the works (Fig 1.17).

On a few large gasworks, coke ovens were adopted which could make gas on a larger scale (Fig 1.18). In the 1950s it was realised that the quality and quantity of gas coals were diminishing; the last conventional coal gasworks was built at White Lund, Morecambe, in 1958 (Fig 1.19). The industry switched to producing gas from refinery by-products such as liquid petroleum gas (LPG), and the old coal gasworks were cleared away and replaced by new gasworks, such as those built at Cadwell Lane, Hitchin (Fig 1.20).

Fig 1.2
Cloughfold, Lancashire, 1909. Rossendale Union Gas Company, view of the gasholders behind Newchurch Mill.
[© IGEM]

Fig 1.3
Portrait of Friedrich Winzer, who promoted the Gas Light and Coke Company, 1830.
[© LGM]

Fig 1.4
Monkseaton, North Tyneside c 1920. Lit by Sugg's upright Littleton lamps.
[© IGEM]

Fig 1.5
Beckton, London, 1881. View of the gasworks from the clock tower.
[© IGEM]

Fig 1.6
Beckton, London, 1926. Bank of retorts in the large retort houses.
[© IGEM]

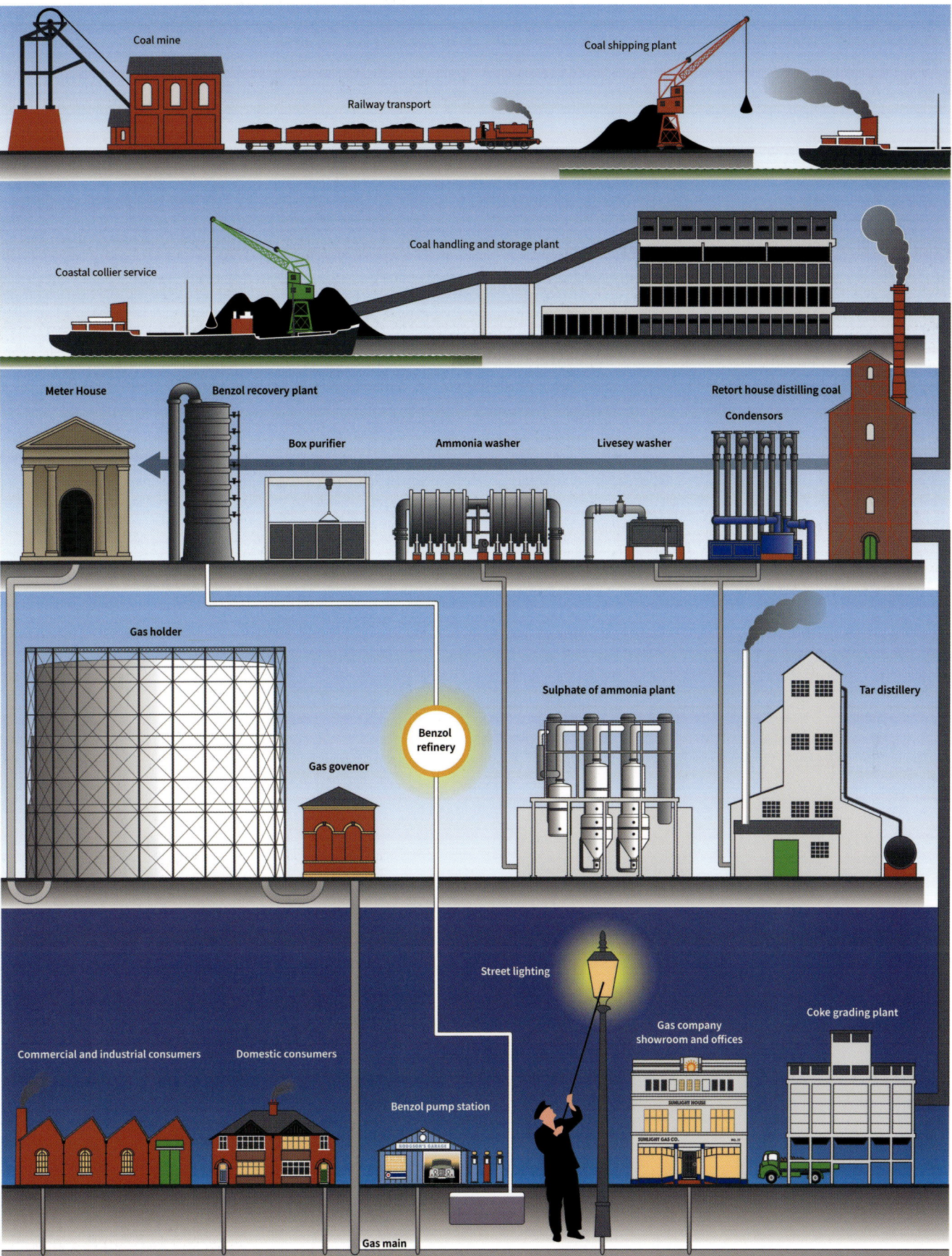

Fig 1.7
The whole gas production process from the coal mine to the delivery to the customer.
[© Historic England based on an illustration by Professor Russell Thomas]

Fig 1.8
Beckton, London, 1926. Condensers, washers and scrubbers.
[© IGEM]

Fig 1.9
Beckton, London, 1926. A bank of rotary scrubbers in front of spiral-guided gasholders.
[© IGEM]

Fig 1.10
Alresford, Hampshire, 1928. The manager and staff of the gasworks.
[© IGEM]

Fig 1.11
Blakeney, Gloucestershire, 1933.
[© IGEM]

Fig 1.12
Sherbourne, Dorset, 1956. Condensers, washers and scrubbers.
[© IGEM]

Fig 1.13
Fakenham, Norfolk, 2015. The gas museum, the last surviving gasworks in England.
[© Historic England Archive 29328/003]

I INTRODUCTION

Fig 1.14
Schematic diagram of a frame-guided gasholder in a below-ground tank, which shows the water seal and how the telescopic lifts engage as the gasholder fills with gas, 2023.
[© Russell Thomas]

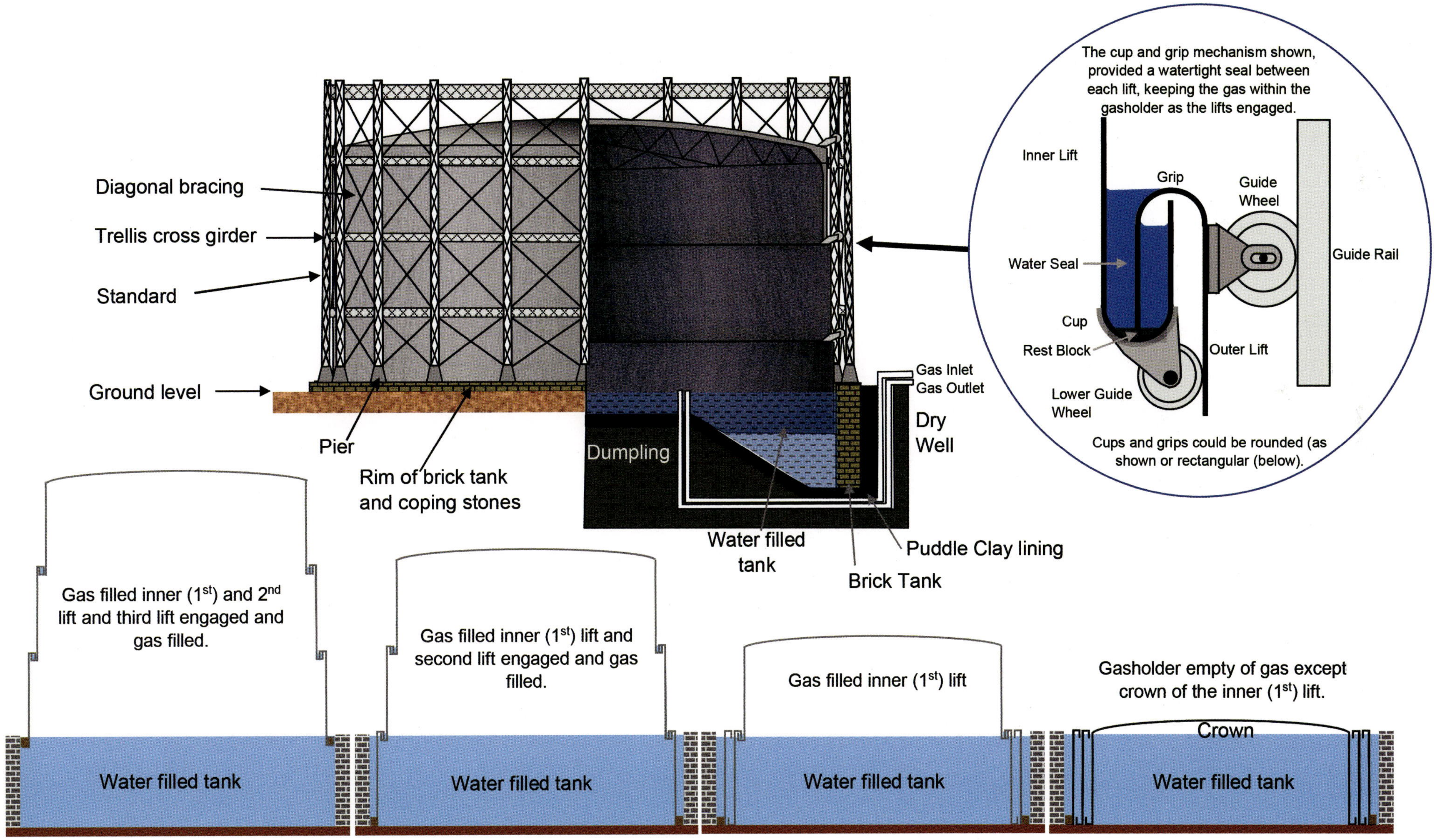

Fig 1.15
Bath, c 1950. Aerial photograph of the gasworks.
[© IGEM]

Fig 1.16
Windsor, Berkshire, 1947. The gasworks under flood water.
[© Historic England Archive EAW003702]

Fig 1.17
Northampton, 1951. The Peckett locomotive 'Norman' at the gasworks.
[© IGEM]

Fig 1.18
Beckton, London, 1926. Coke oven plant.
[© IGEM]

1 INTRODUCTION

Fig 1.19
White Lund, Morecambe, Lancashire, 1958. The last coal gasworks.
[© IGEM]

Fig 1.20
Hitchin, Hertfordshire, c 1970. The new gasworks.
[© IGEM]

2 Evolution of gasholders

The gasholder was an integral part of the gasworks from the start. The French scientist Antoine Lavoisier developed the gazomètre as a scientific instrument for measuring gas for his experiments. Boulton and Watt's engineers adapted and enlarged it to provide storage for coal gas.

The gasholder design consisted of a water-filled tank and a vessel storing gas (lift), sealed at one end, and inverted over the water and counterweighted. This design was adopted by Samuel Clegg in the gasworks he built in 1811 at Dolphinholme, Lancashire (Figs 2.1 and 2.2).

Early designs were rectangular or cylindrical and had a heavy construction built from iron and wood. This created too much gas pressure which had to be offset by counterweights.

Samuel Clegg developed two innovative designs, a rotating gasholder and a tent-shaped gasholder. Both had drawbacks, so Clegg stuck with the conventional design. All three designs featured in Christian Accum's *Practical Treatise on Gas Light* (Fig 2.3).

The cylindrical gasholder design was favoured and adopted in future gasholders (Fig 2.4), and the use of lighter construction materials allowed counterweights to be reduced and eventually eliminated.

Safety concerns led members of the Royal Society to recommend that gasholders should be housed in buildings (Figs 2.5 and 2.6) and a limit placed on their size. Although initially adopted, these rules were soon abandoned.

Gasholders which used columns to support and guide the lift as it moved up and down were adopted. These columns generally took the form of cast iron tripod frames (Fig 2.7).

The water-filled tanks could be built above or below ground level. Those above ground were originally made from wood but later replaced by tanks made from cast iron sections bolted together as in Fig 2.8.

As demand for gas increased, gas storage became a problem. Tait, Nicholson and Hutchinson all developed systems where multiple lifts could be connected in a telescopic fashion as shown in Fig 1.14. Hutchinson's example is shown in Fig 2.9.

As the capacity of gasholders increased, so did the size of the columns. Larger tripod frames were constructed with cross bracing at the top to make them more stable (Fig 2.10).

The tripods were replaced by cylindrical cast iron columns, following classical designs and sometimes ornate (Fig 2.11). These were replaced by cast iron standards, which were in turn gradually replaced by wrought iron, which John Paddon and George Trewby used to construct the lattice framing of their gasholders at Hove (Fig 2.12) and Bethnal Green (Fig 2.13).

Wrought iron was replaced by steel in the construction of the whole gasometer. The lighter frames, which adopted new principles of construction, allowed bigger gasholders with multiple lifts, the lifts being guided with guide wheels (Fig 2.14).

The advent of frameless gasholders gave rise to spiral-guided (Fig 2.15) and wire-rope-guided gasholders, the former being the most successful, with the design adopted for most 20th-century gasholders.

As gasworks evolved, sites often had different forms of gasholder, as can be seen in the photographs of Ryde (Fig 2.16), Beckton (Fig 2.17) and Battersea (Fig 2.18).

Another development to increase the capacity of a gasholder was the flying lift. This was where one or more lifts could extend above the frame of the gasholder as in Fig 2.19.

The final evolution of the gasholder was the high-pressure bullet tanks, special reinforced vessels which could store gas at high pressures (Fig 2.20).

Fig 2.1
Dolphinholme, Lancashire. An artist's impression of Samuel Clegg's gasholder.
[© John Vallender Historic England]

Fig 2.2
Dolphinholme, Lancashire, 2019. The gasholder tank and counterweight.
[© Matthew Bristow]

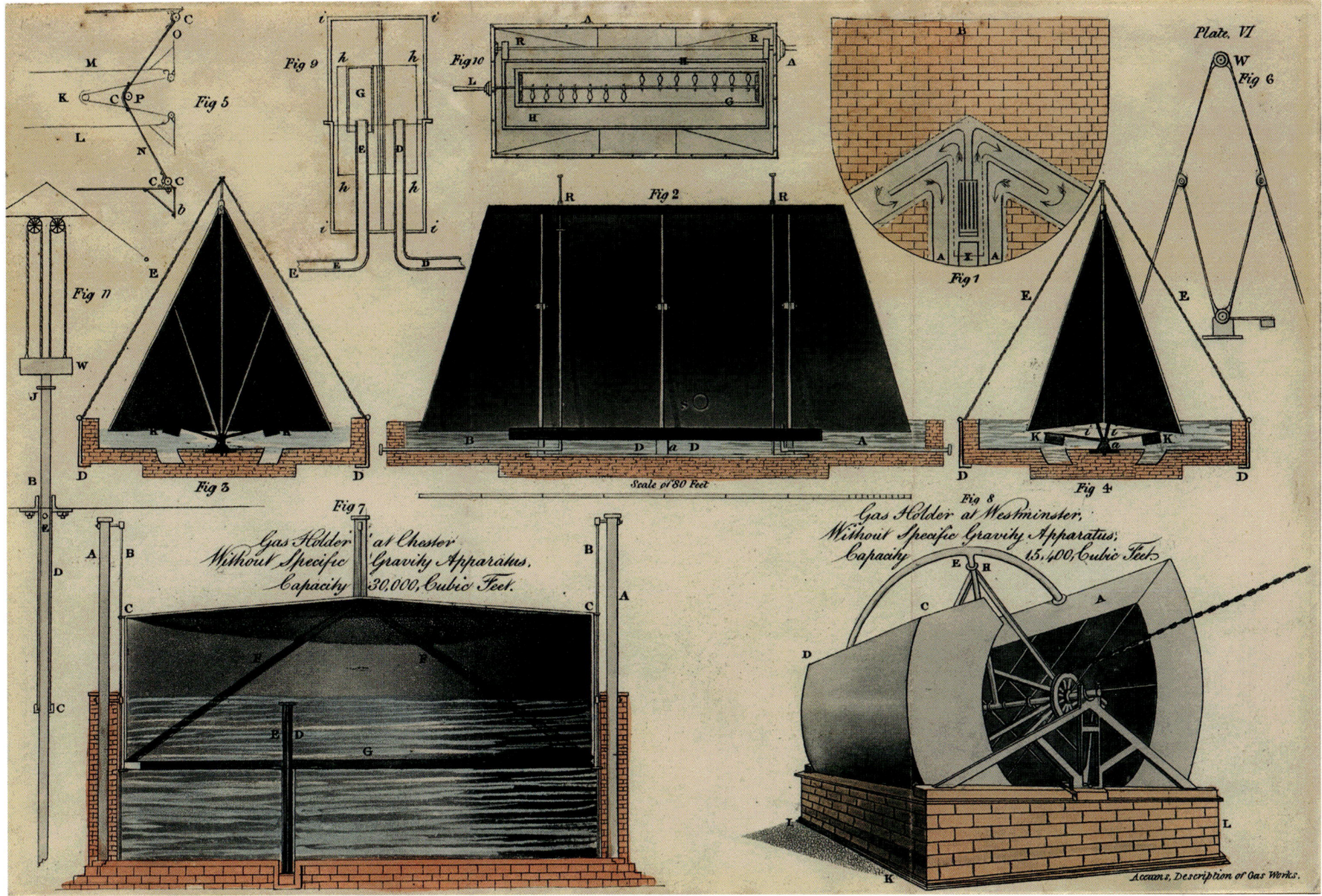

Fig 2.3
Christian Accum's *Practical Treatise on Gas Light*, 1817.
Designs of different types of gasholders.
[IGEM]

Fig 2.4
Smethwick, West Midlands, 1903. A gasholder, which was still in use at the Avery works, Smethwick. It was originally thought to have been designed by William Murdoch but is now believed to have been built later.
[© NGA]

Fig 2.5
Saltisford, Warwick, 2016. The surviving gasholder houses.
[© Historic England Archive 33260/013]

Fig 2.6
Oxford, 1880. The gasworks with a gasholder house located between two column-guided gasholders with counterweights.
[© Historic England Archive CC68/00038]

Fig 2.7
Fulham, London, 2019. Gasholder No 2 using tripod columns, the oldest surviving gasholder in the world, dating to 1830.
[© Historic England Archive DP413764]

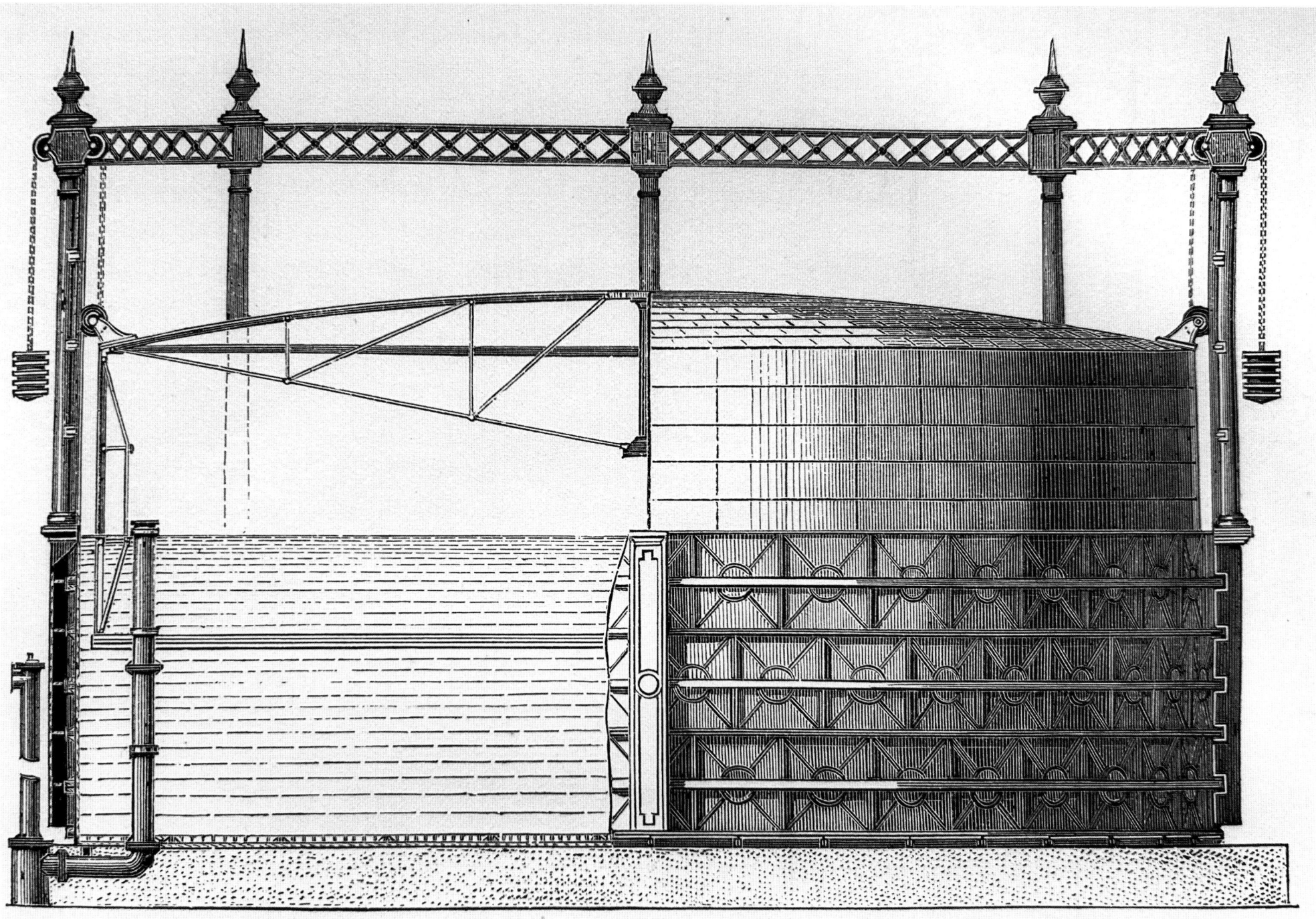

Fig 2.8
A print of a single-lift gasholder in a cast iron tank with counterweights, 1879.
[Newbigging and Fewtrell, 1879]

Fig 2.9
Hutchinson's design for a telescopic gasholder, 1836.
[Mechanics Magazine]

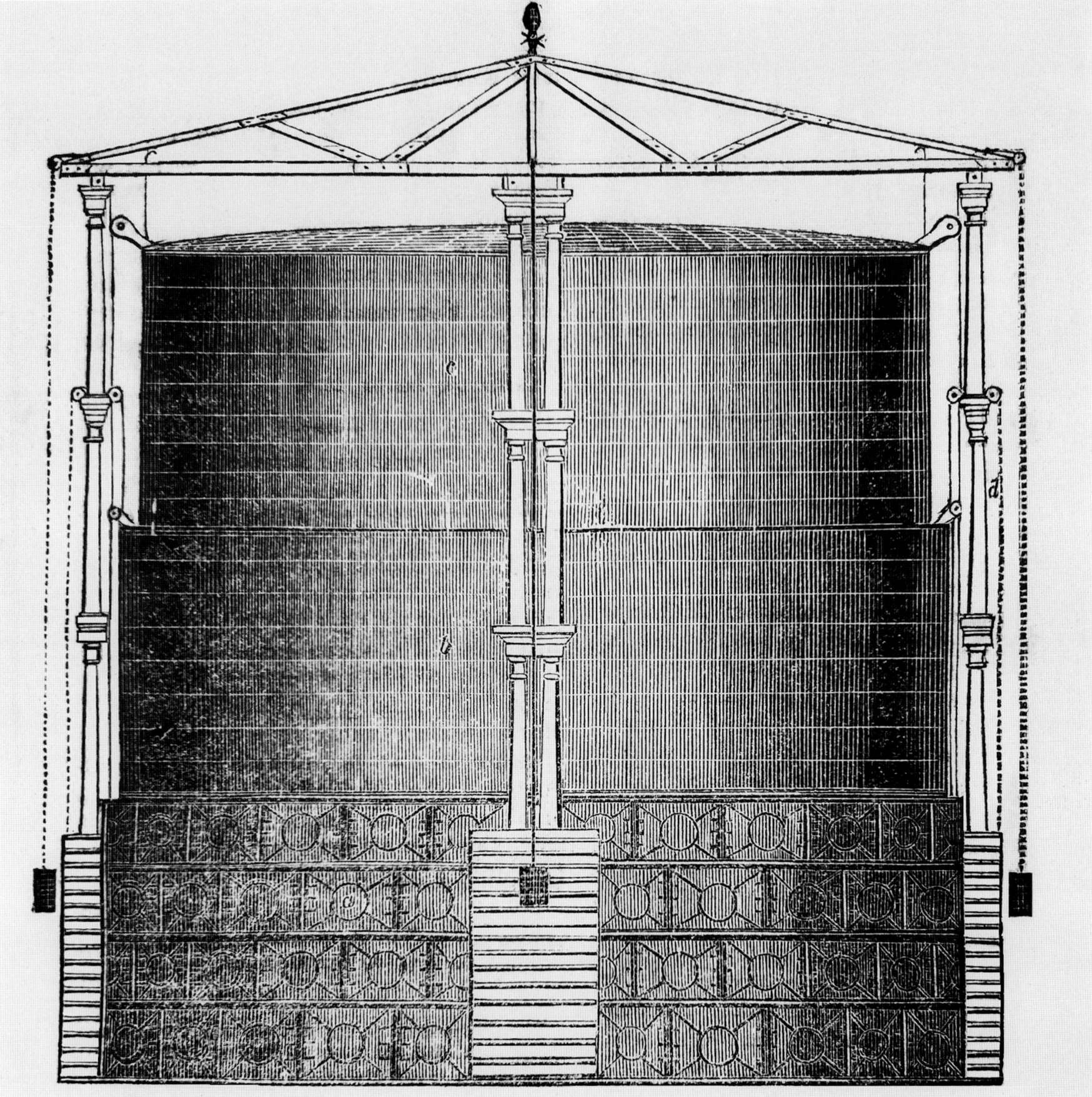

Fig 2.10
Fulham, London, 1926. No 4 tripod gasholder.
[© IGEM]

Fig 2.11
South Shields, Tyne and Wear, 1989. The column-guided No 1 gasholder.
[© NGA]

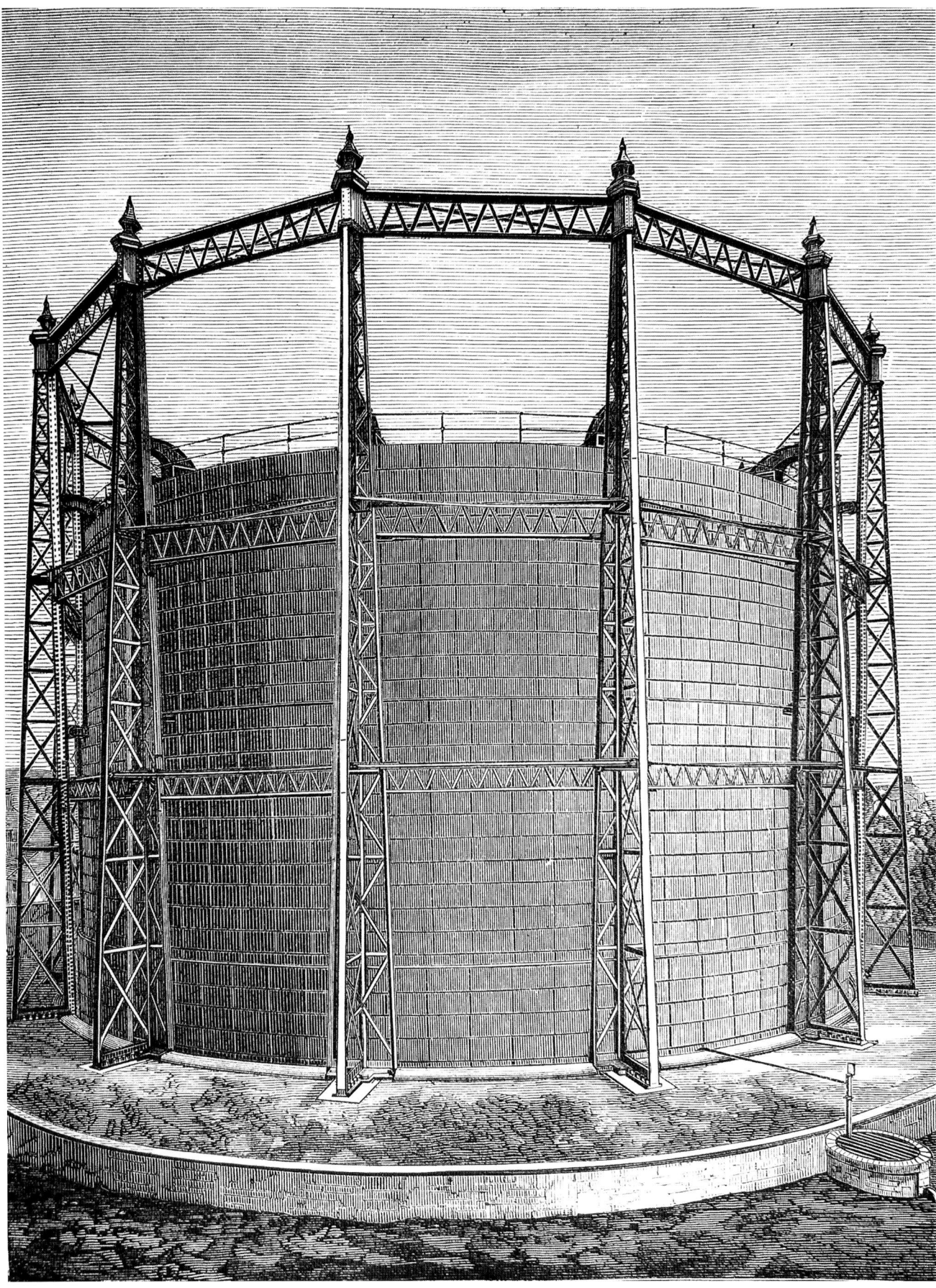

Fig 2.12
Hove, East Sussex, 1876. Paddon's frame-guided gasholder.
[Newbigging and Fewtrell, 1879]

Fig 2.13
Bethnal Green, London 1934. Four gasholders, including the largest, George Trewby's No 5 gasholder.
[© IGEM]

Fig 2.14
Blackburn, Lancashire, 2016. Stacked guide wheels on the large frame-guided No 3 gasholder.
[© Historic England Archive DP186292]

Fig 2.15
Millbrook, Southampton, 1960. Three-lift spiral-guided gasholder.
[© IGEM]

GASHOLDERS: A HISTORY IN PICTURES

Fig 2.17
Beckton, London, 1926. Central Avenue, Beckton, gasworks, with a variety of column-, frame- and spiral-guided gasholders.
[© IGEM]

Fig 2.16
Ryde, Isle of Wight, c 1920. A collection of column-, frame- and spiral-guided gasholders.
[© IGEM]

Fig 2.18
Battersea, London, 2010. The site featured a column, frame, spiral and waterless gasholder.
[© Historic England Archive 26622/025]

Fig 2.19
Neepsend, Sheffield, c 1950. A flying lift fitted to a frame-guided gasholder.
[© LGM]

Fig 2.20
Rayleigh, Essex, 1945. A frame-guided gasholder, a grounded spiral-guided gasholder and a high-pressure bullet tank.
[© IGEM]

Fig 3.1
Fulham, London, 1926. No 2 and No 4 gasholders (tripod-guided) and No 3 and No 5 gasholders (column-guided).
[© IGEM]

3 Column-guided gasholders

The very earliest surviving gasholder in the United Kingdom, the No 2 gasholder at Fulham, in London, dates back to Georgian times. Typical of its time, it used tripod columns formed from cast iron to guide the gasholder. These used rods on the inside of the tripod which guided the lift by means of an eyelet attached to the lift which moved up and down on the rods. As tripod gasholders grew larger, the tripods were braced together using iron bars (Fig 3.1).

Tripods were not the only designs. For some smaller gasholders, a single central cast iron column was used to guide the lift up and down, with wheels attached to the top and bottom of the lift, whereas on small gasworks simple iron columns guided the lift with the use of counterweights (Fig 3.2).

Between the 1840s and 1890s, most large gasholders adopted a design composed of a ring of cast iron columns joined around the circumference by horizontal girders. Some used a single tier of girders, such as at Preston (Fig 3.3) or Fulham (Figs 3.4 and 3.5).

It was typical for these types of gasholders to have very ornate features such as decorative roses (Fig 3.3) and filigree lattice work (Fig 3.4). The columns used in these types of gasholders were constructed from cast iron. On their inside (facing the lift), guide rails were attached, within which wheels fixed by arms on the top and bottom of the lift would run to ensure the rigid guiding of the lift, so that it would remain level and not jam (Fig 3.5).

Larger gasholders such as those shown at Beckton, London (Fig 3.6), and Bow Common, London (Fig 3.7), had two tiers of girders and maintained the same highly decorative features, the columns on the Bow Common gasholders having unusual square columns.

The No 4 and No 5 gasholders at the Kennington Oval, London (Fig 3.8), were embellished with phoenixes on the columns (Fig 3.9), which were the emblem of the company that built them, the Phoenix GLCC.

The engineering details of a two-lift gasholder design used at the Linacre gasworks in Bootle, Liverpool, can be seen in Fig 3.10, with the actual gasholders visible in Fig 3.11.

Not all column-guided gasholders were highly decorative, such as the examples built at the gasworks in Scarborough, shown in Fig 3.12.

The finest column-guided gasholder, according to the notable engineer George Livesey, was the three-lift column-guided gasholder designed by William Mann and built by Westwood & Wright for the City of London GLCC works at Blackfriars, London, in 1861 (Fig 3.13).

Mann's gasholder included diagonal tie bars to provide extra stability, which was adopted on most other three-tier column-guided gasholders. The ornamentation ranged from simple designs built at Salford (Fig 3.14), through to more ornate examples built at Carlisle (Fig 3.15) and Portsmouth (Fig 3.16).

The gasholders built at Bromley-by-Bow, London, are a fine example of the ornate column-guided gasholders built for the Imperial GLCC by Westwood & Wright. They are a unique surviving group of column-guided gasholders (Figs 3.17–3.19).

The first gasholders to be reused in a redevelopment project in England were the four gasholders at Kings Cross. They were dismantled in 2001 and gradually re-erected from 2013 (Figs 3.20 and 3.21).

Due to the heavy weight of the cast iron columns and the foundations they required, column-guided gasholders reached a theoretical limit to their size, beyond which new designs would be required to build larger gasholders.

Fig 3.2
Gunnislake, Cornwall, c 1950. A simple single-lift column-guided gasholder.
[© NGA]

Fig 3.3
Preston, Lancashire, 2016. Ornate column-guided gasholder.
[© Historic England Archive DP186260]

Fig 3.4
Fulham, London, 1926. The highly ornate column-guided No 5 gasholder.
[© IGEM]

Fig 3.5
Fulham, London, 1926. Details of the columns and guide wheels on No 5 gasholder.
[© IGEM]

Fig 3.6
Beckton, London, 1881. No 5 gasholder, using ornate cast iron columns.
[© IGEM]

Fig 3.7
Bow Common, London, 1872. Ornate column-guided gasholder.
[© IGEM]

Fig 3.8
Kennington, London, 2017. No 4 and No 5 gasholders.
[© Historic England Archive DP182532]

Fig 3.9
Kennington, London, 2017. Detail of the Phoenix emblem on the No 4 and No 5 gasholders.
[© Historic England Archive DP413890]

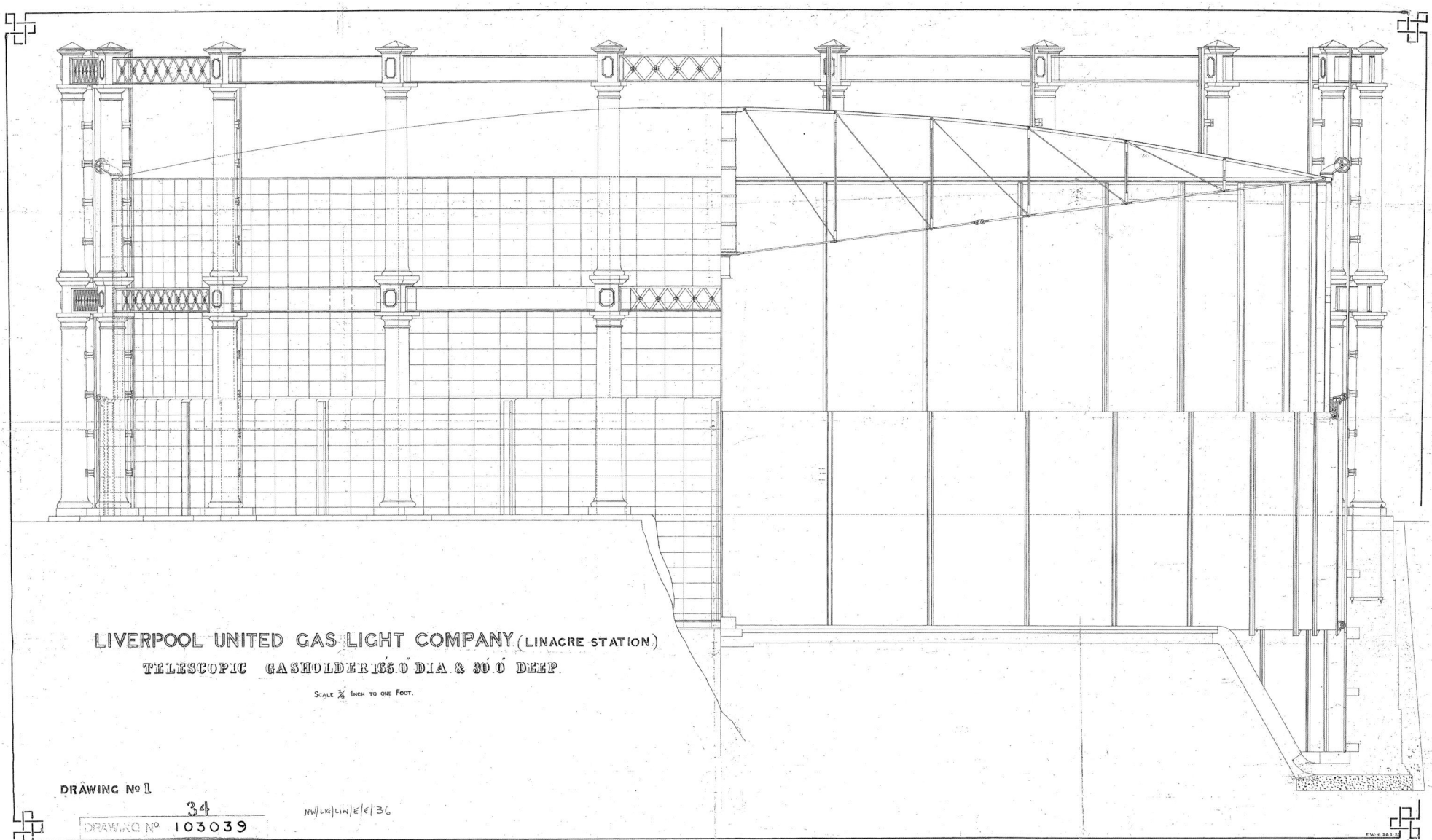

Fig 3.10
Bootle, Liverpool, 1882. Engineering drawing of the two-lift gasholder design adopted at the Linacre gasworks.
[© NGA]

Fig 3.11
Bootle, Liverpool, c 1950. Two-lift column-guided gasholder.
[© NGA]

Fig 3.12
Scarborough, Yorkshire, 1957. Two-lift column-guided gasholder.
[© IGEM]

3 COLUMN-GUIDED GASHOLDERS

Fig 3.13
Blackfriars, London. William Mann's three-lift gasholder.
[Newbigging and Fewtrell, 1879]

GASHOLDERS: A HISTORY IN PICTURES

Fig 3.14
Salford, Manchester, 2016. Column-guided gasholder.
[© Historic England Archive DP186269]

Fig 3.15
Rome Street, Carlisle, 2002. Column-guided gasholder.
[© Larry D Brown. Source: Historic England Archive IOE01/08621/23]

GASHOLDERS: A HISTORY IN PICTURES

Fig 3.16
Rudmore, Portsmouth, 1983.
Column-guided gasholder.
[© IGEM]

3 COLUMN-GUIDED GASHOLDERS

Fig 3.17
Bromley-by-Bow, London, 2021. Looking north across the bell of gasholder No 1.
[© Historic England Archive DP413977]

GASHOLDERS: A HISTORY IN PICTURES

Fig 3.18
Bromley-by-Bow, London, 2021. Detail of guide frames and decorative ironwork on gasholder.
[© Historic England Archive DP413965]

Fig 3.19
Bromley-by-Bow, London, 2021. Detail of decorative ironwork on gasholder.
[© Historic England Archive DP413971]

Fig 3.20
Kings Cross, London, 1989. The gasholders from the canal while operational.
[© Historic England Archive DD001262]

3 COLUMN-GUIDED GASHOLDERS

Fig 3.21
Kings Cross, London, 2001. Gasholder No 8 being dismantled.
[© Historic England Archive AA024963]

4 Frame-guided gasholders

By 1880, the design of gasholders using cast iron columns had reached the maximum size achievable within the constraints of this design. The design of gasholders then developed with a period of great innovation. Heavy columns were replaced by lighter standards, at first made from cast iron, then wrought iron and finally steel.

Vitruvius Wyatt, engineer to the GLCC in 1876, adopted lighter I-section cast iron standards with two tiers of girders in a design used at Kensal Green, Beckton (Fig 4.1) and Fulham (Fig 4.2) in London.

In 1876 wrought iron was used in the design of the standards by Robert and Harry Jones on gasholder No 1 at Poplar gasworks in London (Fig 4.3) and by John Paddon at Hove gasworks (*see* Fig 2.12). Poplar gasholder No 1 used tapering T-section standards with lattice buttressing. Paddon's gasholder at Hove used tapering standards constructed from T sections and lattice webbing. It also featured Paddon wind ties (overlapping bars or cables, which connected the tops of alternate standards), which strengthened the gasholder by sharing the load between the different standards.

Wrought iron standards were also used in Corbett Woodall's design of gasholder No 1 built at the Kennington Oval, London (Fig 4.4). Gasholders No 7 and No 8 at Sydenham (Fig 4.5) used a similar design with tapered wrought iron lattice standards. Later gasholders adopted steel rather than wrought iron.

The standards were spaced around the gasholder tank at a distance of between 4.9 and 9 metres and were braced horizontally by girders and diagonally by ties. The girders were built up from wrought iron or steel sections, while the diagonal ties were typically made from plain, round or flat steel bars. The tapered lattice girders were widely adopted on gasholders, replacing columns, with some fine examples provided in Figs 4.6–4.13.

Box girders were also adopted for standards used on gasholders. George Trewby of the GLCC used them on the Bethnal Green No 5, Kensal Green No 6 and Beckton No 9 gasholders. He used steel for the construction of the whole crown and the principal members of the guide frame on the latter two gasholders. This design was also widely adopted with examples shown in Figs 4.14–4.17.

In some cases, simpler frames were constructed from rolled steel joists (RSJ) or equivalent used as standards. These were again connected by horizontal girders and diagonal ties, with examples shown in Figs 4.18–4.20.

The early guide frames used standards in a similar way to columns, forming the standards into a rigid frame using horizontal beams. George Livesey developed the concept of the whole guide frame acting as one cylindrical member cantilevered from the ground. The first gasholder to use this design was the listed gasholder No 13 at Old Kent Road, London (*see* Figs 11.16 and 11.17). It used much lighter standards compared to other gasholders of the time. The standards were connected together using diagonal ties and horizontal struts instead of girders, forming a strong cylindrical frame.

George, with his brother Frank Livesey, developed the concept further in the huge No 1 (*see* Fig 11.18) and No 2 (*see* Fig 11.19) gasholders built at the South Metropolitan Gas Company works at East Greenwich, London, from 1886. Gasholder No 2 was the largest gasholder to have been built on a gasworks in the United Kingdom; it held 12 million ft^3. The upper two lifts extended above the height of the frame. Croydon gasholder No 5 (Fig 4.21) adopted the same principles as Livesey's design.

This lattice shell concept was further adapted by Samuel Cutler and Sons, who developed Cutler's patented guide framing in 1888, a design which consisted of vertical standards braced by diagonal triangulated framing forming equilateral triangles (Fig 4.22). Horizontal girders were only used at the top of the frame.

Fig 4.1
Beckton, London, 1881. Gasholders No 7 and No 8 with cast iron frames.
[© IGEM]

4 FRAME-GUIDED GASHOLDERS

Fig 4.3
Poplar, London, 2016. Gasholder No 1.
[© Historic England Archive DP183487]

Fig 4.2
Fulham, London, 2008. Gasholder No 7 with cast iron frame.
[© Historic England Archive DP413736]

Fig 4.4
Kennington, London, 2021. Gasholder No 1.
[© Historic England Archive DP413905]

Fig 4.5
Sydenham, London, 2017. Gasholders No 7 and No 8.
[© Historic England Archive 33089/026]

Fig 4.6
Wellingborough, Northamptonshire, 1967.
Frame-guided gasholder.
[© NGA]

Fig 4.7
Bourne Valley, Poole, Dorset, 2001.
[© Historic England Archive AA024925]

Fig 4.8
Reading, Berkshire, 1905. Gasholder No 4.
[© IGEM]

4 FRAME-GUIDED GASHOLDERS

Fig 4.9
Bradford Road, Manchester, 2023.
[© Jam Butty Photography and Video and IPB Communications]

Fig 4.10
Bradford Road, Manchester, 2023.
[© Jam Butty Photography and Video and IPB Communications]

4 FRAME-GUIDED GASHOLDERS

Fig 4.11
Eastbourne, East Sussex, 2014. Frame-guided gasholders No 3 and No 4.
[© Historic England Archive DP263005]

Fig 4.12
Wavertree, Liverpool, 2016. Two frame-guided gasholders.
[© Historic England Archive DP197007]

Fig 4.13
West Ham, London, 1965. Frame-guided gasholder.
[© Historic England Archive AA100187]

GASHOLDERS: A HISTORY IN PICTURES

Fig 4.15
Southampton, Hampshire, 1923. Gasholder No 9.
[© IGEM]

Fig 4.14
New Southgate, London, 1978.
Frame-guided gasholder.
[© IGEM]

Fig 4.16
Redheugh, Gateshead, 2016. Frame-guided gasholder reflected in a puddle.
[© John Morton]

Fig 4.17
Redheugh, Gateshead, 1989.
[© NGA]

4 FRAME-GUIDED GASHOLDERS

Fig 4.18
Helston, Cornwall, c 1950. Small frame-guided gasholder using RSJ for standards.
[© NGA]

4 FRAME-GUIDED GASHOLDERS

Fig 4.19
Bath, 2014. A view through the framing of gasholder No 3.
[© Oliver Lancaster]

Fig 4.20
Aldershot, Hampshire, 1969. Gasholders No 3 (front) with flying lift and No 4.
[© IGEM]

4 FRAME-GUIDED GASHOLDERS

Fig 4.21
Croydon, London, 2017. Gasholder No 5.
[© Historic England Archive 33089/031]

Fig 4.22
Dartford, Kent, 2001. Cutler's patented frame-guided gasholder No 3.
[© Historic England Archive AA022867]

Fig 5.1
Hitchin, Hertfordshire, 1949. Three-lift gasholder in low cloud.
[© Historic England Archive EAW020887]

5 Spiral-guided gasholders

The spiral-guided gasholder was an ingenious design (Fig 5.1). It was the most successful of several designs which appeared at the end of the 19th century which removed the need for an external frame. The concept was originally proposed by Webber, evolving into the design patented in 1887 by Gadd and Mason of Manchester.

The first example of this type of gasholder was built in 1890 at the Northwich gasworks, Cheshire. The guide rails were at first placed on the inside of the lifts as shown in Fig 5.2. The guide rails were later placed on the outside of the lifts.

The guiding system, composed of helical guide rails, curved around the lift at an incline of 45°. The lifts were reinforced with vertical stiffeners and plates behind the spiral guide rails, removing the need for framing. The spiral guide rails were gripped between pairs of rollers held within the guide carriage as seen in Fig 5.3.

When filled with gas as shown in Fig 5.4, these structures were highly visible features on the landscape, especially after the gasworks had been demolished (Figs 5.4 and 5.5) or when located on gasholder stations (Fig 5.6).

When built in below-ground tanks and empty of gas, the spiral-guided gasholder was barely visible to the public, with little protruding above the tank as shown in Figs 5.7 and 5.8.

The gasholders were often painted using a colour scheme so that they blended into the surrounding environment when inflated, such as that used at Stanmore in Fig 5.9.

The construction detail of a two-lift spiral-guided gasholder in an above-ground tank built by engineers Firth Blakeley is shown in Fig 5.10, with the gasholder shown in Fig 5.11.

The guide rails could all be angled in a sequence of opposing directions (Fig 5.12) or the same direction (Fig 5.13).

The guide carriages were mounted at regular intervals on the top edge of the gasholder tank and on the top of each subsequent lift, except for the inner lift (Fig 5.14).

The spiral-guided gasholder came to dominate the type of gasholder built in the 20th century. They were often built within the tanks of former column- and frame-guided gasholders. Above-ground steel tanks were used where the ground conditions were unsuitable, such as a high water table, for a below-ground tank, as shown in Fig 5.15.

Partially below-ground tanks were used, as was the case of one of the two largest ever spiral-guided gasholders (capacity of 8 million ft^3) built by Newton Chambers at Meadowhall, Sheffield (Fig 5.16).

Gasholders provided an advertising opportunity, with advertisements painted on the inner lift of the gasholder, visible from a long distance when inflated (Figs 5.17 and 5.18).

Spiral-guided gasholders came in all dimensions, from narrow and tall (Fig 5.19) to wide and squat (Fig 5.20). They were also occasionally painted with a number scale to indicate the amount of gas stored (Figs 5.20 and 5.21).

Fig 5.2
From an advertisement by R&J Dempster of Manchester, c 1890. Print of an early spiral-guided gasholder design.
[IGEM]

5 SPIRAL-GUIDED GASHOLDERS

Fig 5.3
Beckton, London, 1941. Spiral guide rail and guide carriage of the reconstructed No 2 gasholder.
[© IGEM]

Fig 5.4
Weymouth, Dorset, 2000. Three-lift spiral-guided gasholder.
[© Historic England Archive AA003410]

5 SPIRAL-GUIDED GASHOLDERS

Fig 5.5
Boston, Lincolnshire, c 1970. Three-lift spiral-guided gasholder.
[© NGA]

Fig 5.6
Horton Road, Gloucester, 1938. Four-lift spiral-guided gasholder.
[© Historic England Archive EPW058600]

Fig 5.7
Bishop Auckland, County Durham, 1991. Grounded spiral-guided gasholder, showing the guide carriages on the tank.
[© Historic England Archive AA004390]

Fig 5.8
Bishop Bridge Road, Norwich, 2018. Overhead view of a grounded spiral-guided gasholder.
[© AtkinsRéalis]

Fig 5.9
Stanmore, London, 1975. Three spiral-guided gasholders.
[© IGEM]

5 SPIRAL-GUIDED GASHOLDERS

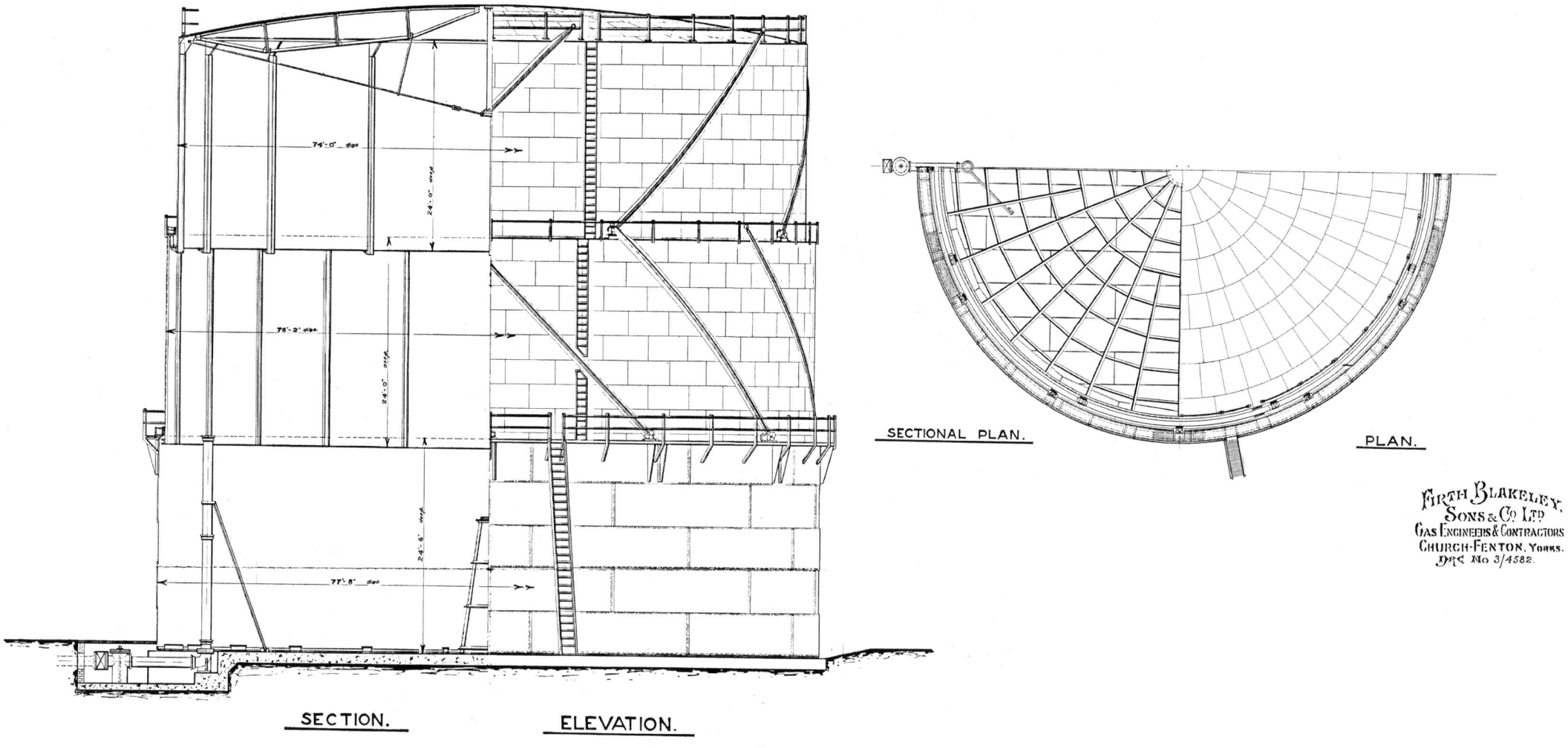

Fig 5.10
St Helens, Isle of Wight. Engineering drawing for a two-lift spiral-guided gasholder.
[© IGEM]

Fig 5.11
St Helens, Isle of Wight, 1956. Spiral-guided gasholder as depicted in Fig 5.10.
[© IGEM]

Fig 5.12
Willington Quay, North Tyneside, 2007. Spiral-guided gasholder.
[© John Morton]

Fig 5.13
Neepsend, Sheffield, c 1970. Spiral-guided gasholder in a steel tank.
[© NGA]

Fig 5.14
Neepsend, Sheffield, c 1950. Construction of the spiral-guided gasholder shown in Fig 5.13.
[© LGM]

Fig 5.15
Kingston, Isle of Wight, 1968. Two above-ground spiral-guided gasholders and a small frame-guided gasholder.
[© IGEM]

5 SPIRAL-GUIDED GASHOLDERS

Fig 5.16
Meadowhall, Sheffield, c 1970. Two huge spiral-guided gasholders.
[© NGA]

Fig 5.17
Cannon Street, Middlesbrough, c 1930. Spiral-guided gasholder in a steel tank.
[© IGEM]

Fig 5.18
Birkshall, Bradford, 1938. Spiral-guided gasholder.
[© IGEM]

Fig 5.19
Isle of Portland, Dorset, 1954. Three-lift spiral-guided gasholder in a steel tank, built by R&J Dempster.
[© IGEM]

Fig 5.20
Wareham, Dorset, c 1950. Gasholder No 4, with numerical gauge to indicate the amount of gas within the gasholder.
[© IGEM]

Fig 5.21
Fareham, Hampshire, 1948. Two spiral-guided gasholders.
[© IGEM]

6 Waterless gasholders

Waterless gasholders were developed to remove the costly and complex exercise of building a water tank. Attempts were made in the early 19th century by engineers such as Samuel Clegg and William Knapton, but the construction materials were not durable, and they soon failed.

The construction of the first effective waterless gasholder occurred at Augsburg Gasworks, Germany, in 1915. It was developed by the German company Maschinenfabrik Augsburg-Nürnberg AG and known in the United Kingdom as a MAN gasholder. The best-known example built in the United Kingdom was constructed at Battersea (Figs 6.1–6.3).

Waterless gasholders had a fixed outer shell, which maintained a constant size. The shell of a MAN gasholder had a polygonal shape (Fig 6.3).

The gas was stored within the shell beneath an airtight piston sealed by tar or oil (grease in the case of a Klönne gasholder), seen detailed in Fig 6.4.

The first MAN gasholder built in the United Kingdom was at Ipswich, Suffolk, in 1927 (Fig 6.5). The GLCC built many of these gasholders; their first was built at Staines, with others built in London at Kensal Green, Woodford (Fig 6.6), Southall (Fig 6.7), Battersea (see Figs 6.1–6.3), Harrow and Brentford.

The MAN gasholder at Southall (Fig 6.7), was a well-known air navigation landmark. It had the Letters LH and an arrow painted on it indicating Heathrow Airport, after a pilot had landed a Boeing 707 at RAF Northolt in 1960, following confusion with the MAN gasholder at Harrow.

The construction of the MAN gasholder at Swan Village, West Bromwich gasworks for the Birmingham Corporation Gas Department (Fig 6.8) was well documented. As no water tank was required, the shell of the gasholder was built directly onto a concrete slab (Fig 6.9).

From the slab, the shell of the gasholder was built upwards, girders being erected in the position of the corners of the polygon. Between the girders, steel sheets were installed, increasing the rigidity of the structure. As the early stages of construction progressed, the roof of the gasholder would be constructed as would the piston. Both of these would be jacked up the shell as it was extended, as can be seen in Figs 6.10 and 6.11.

The construction of the gasholder was a precise operation which required extensive riveting (Fig 6.12) to secure the gas-tight shell. Skilled labour (Fig 6.13) was required to work in the demanding environment.

The gas was stored below a moving piston, able to rise and fall in the shell guided by rollers fixed to its edge. The piston was accessible by a ladder (Figs 6.14 and 6.15) from the roof and steps and/or a lift on the outside of the shell.

Messrs August Klönne of Dortmund designed a similar waterless gasholder. It used a cylindrical rather than polygonal shell. Ashmore, Benson, Pease and Co Ltd constructed a Klönne gasholder at York Gasworks (Fig 6.16) and its immense size dominated the skyline along with the cathedral (Fig 6.17). The piston was accessed by a lift or rope ladder from the roof (Figure 6.18).

The cylindrical Wiggins gasholder (Fig 6.19) was the last waterless gasholder design to be adopted. Originating from the United States of America, the piston used a rubber membrane to seal the gas within the shell.

The first gasholders to store imported natural gas were Wiggins gasholders built at the Canvey Island Liquefied Natural Gas (LNG) Terminal in Essex (Fig 6.20).

Fig 6.1
Battersea, London, 2012. The MAN gasholder.
[© Historic England Archive DP148881]

Fig 6.2
Battersea, London, 1931. Construction of roof frame for the MAN gasholder.
[© IGEM]

Fig 6.3
Battersea, London, 2014. A view from the base looking up the MAN gasholder.
[© Russell Thomas]

Fig 6.4
St Helens, Merseyside, c 1970. An engineering drawing for the MAN gasholder built at St Helens.
[© NGA]

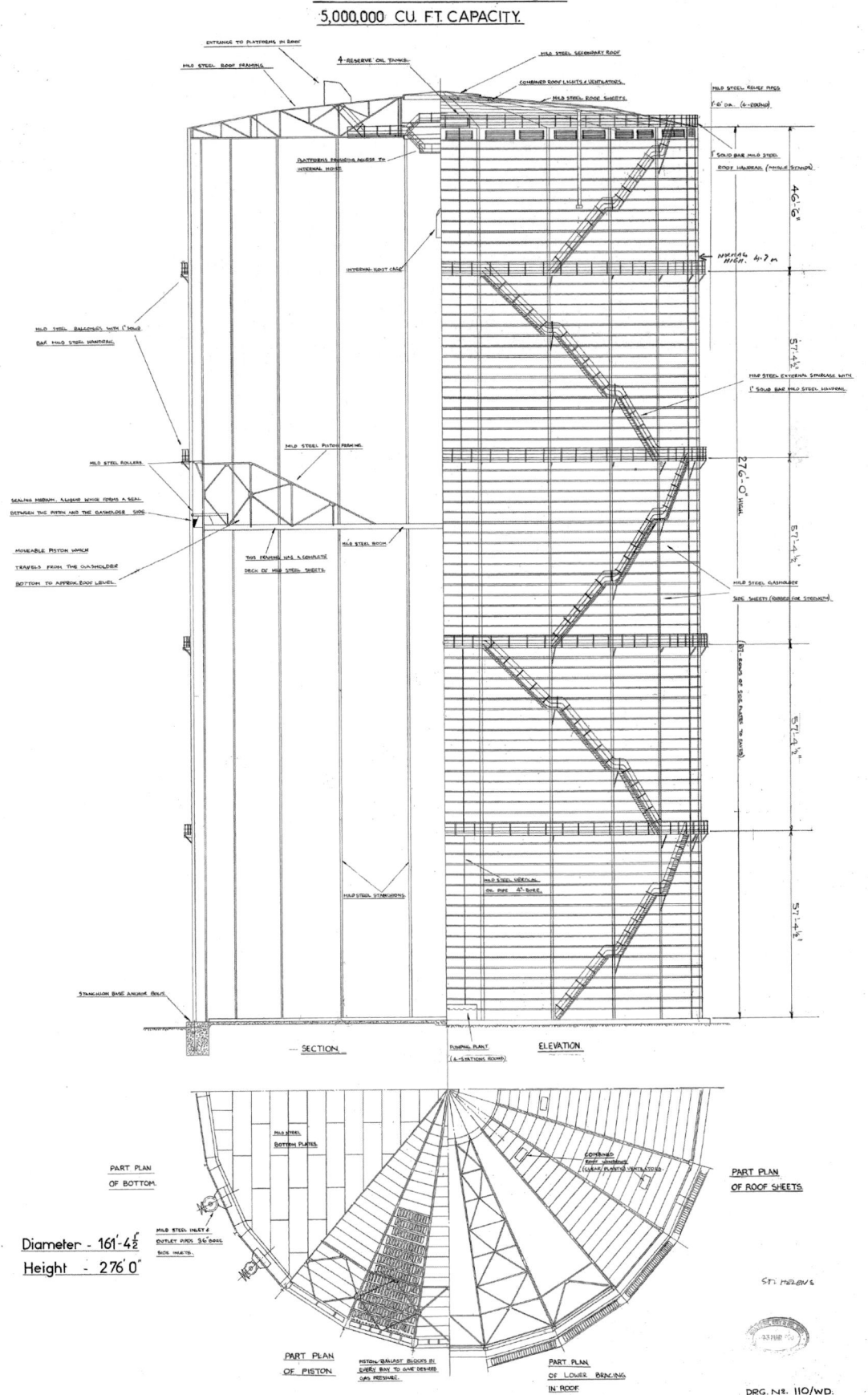

GASHOLDERS: A HISTORY IN PICTURES

Fig 6.5
Ipswich, Suffolk, c 1930. The gasworks with its MAN gasholder.
[© NGA]

Fig 6.6
Woodford, London, 1930. The MAN gasholder built at the Woodford gasworks.
[© IGEM]

Fig 6.7
Southall, London, 1931. An aerial photograph of the MAN gasholder built at Southall.
[© Historic England Archive EPW034912]

Fig 6.8
Swan Village, West Bromwich, 1999. The MAN gasholder.
[© Crown copyright. Source: Historic England Archive BB99/04731]

Fig 6.9
Swan Village, West Bromwich, 1930. Construction of the base slab and initial framing of the MAN gasholder shell.
[© IGEM]

Fig 6.10
Swan Village, West Bromwich, 1930. Construction of the lower section of the MAN gasholder.
[© IGEM]

Fig 6.11
Swan Village, West Bromwich, 1930. Construction of the MAN gasholder from the roof platform.
[© IGEM]

Fig 6.12
Swan Village, West Bromwich, 1930. Riveting the wall panels to the girders on the MAN gasholder.
[© IGEM]

6 WATERLESS GASHOLDERS

Fig 6.13
Swan Village, West Bromwich, 1930. The Clayton Son and Co Ltd construction team.
[© IGEM]

Fig 6.14
Swan Village, West Bromwich, 1930. A view of the ladder-folding system on the piston on the MAN gasholder.
[© IGEM]

Fig 6.15
Swan Village, West Bromwich, 1930. Looking up from the piston towards the top of the MAN gasholder.
[© IGEM]

Fig 6.16
York, 1945. The Klönne gasholder at York gasworks during repainting.
[IGEM]

Fig 6.17
York, 1930. The Klönne gasholder, a prominent feature on the York skyline.
[IGEM]

Fig 6.18
Klönne gasholder, c 1935. The internal lift descending from the roof.
[IGEM]

Fig 6.19
Oakengates, Shropshire, c 1960. Wiggins gasholder.
[© NGA]

Fig 6.20
Canvey Island, Essex, c 1964. Wiggins gasholder built at the LNG terminal.
[© IGEM]

7 High-pressure gasholders

Another form of gasholder was developed which could store the gas at a much higher pressure in a compressed form. The earliest forms of high-pressure gasholder reused the pressure vessels from Lancashire boilers; these were soon replaced by purpose-designed vessels.

The early high-pressure gasholders were formed from steel sections riveted together. One of the earliest examples was installed at the Skipton gasworks in 1933 (Figs 7.1 and 7.2). This gasholder was 32 feet in diameter and 120 feet long and constructed from steel. Such tanks typically operated at a pressure of 3.4 bar.

High-pressure gasholders typically took the form of a bullet tank (long cylindrical vessels with domed ends) or spherical tank. The spherical shape and domed ends prevented stresses forming, as they would if the vessel had sharp corners.

The most famous form of high-pressure gasholder design was the spherical Hortonsphere. It derived its name from Horace Horton, the founder of the American company Chicago Bridge & Iron Company which developed it. An example of this type of gasholder was built on Canvey Island in 1934 and can be seen in Fig 7.3.

This spherical gasholder was later joined by a high-pressure bullet tank. The two vessels on Canvey Island became affectionately known as the Onion and Sausage (Fig 7.4).

Unlike other gasholders, these high-pressure vessels were static, and they had no moving parts. They could receive, store and distribute gas at much higher pressures than other types of gasholders. They supplied more rural areas where it was more cost effective to supply gas through smaller pipes at higher pressure.

Introduced from the 1930s, they provided a stark modernist structure against the older low-pressure column- and frame-guided gasholders. As engineering methods improved, riveted construction (Figs 7.5 and 7.6) was superseded by welded joints (Fig 7.7).

The tanks were delivered in large sections by lorry, which could be a challenge to fit down narrow streets, as it was in Abingdon (Fig 7.8).

Once delivered to site, the tank had to be placed on a specially built stand (Fig 7.9) and the sections welded together (Fig 7.10).

On sites such as Cowley, Oxfordshire (Fig 7.11), and the Isle of Grain in Kent (Fig 7.12), multiple high-pressure bullet tanks were used to provide gas storage.

The pipe array was another method developed for high-pressure gas storage. It used sections of pipeline with domed ends to store gas underground. An example was built at Biggin Hill, near Bromley (Fig 7.13).

High-pressure gasholders were also used to store LPG. LPG was a feedstock in the manufacture of gas in the 1960s prior to the introduction of natural gas (Figs 7.14–7.16).

Prior to the discovery of North Sea natural gas, the United Kingdom had trialled the importation of liquefied natural gas (LNG) by ship from the United States of America to Canvey Island, Essex, in 1959. The gas had to be liquefied by cooling to below –163°C and stored in special insulated tanks. The success of the project led to the expansion of the Canvey Island Terminal, and commercial LNG imports from Algeria started in 1964 (Fig 7.17).

A natural gas pipeline built from Canvey Island to Leeds became the first part of the natural gas network. With the discovery of North Sea natural gas, the United Kingdom decided to convert to natural gas. Special LNG storage sites were constructed at key locations around the country, such as the Isle of Grain (Fig 7.18).

The Grain LNG site has expanded to become a major LNG import terminal (Fig 7.19) which plays a vital role in maintaining the country's energy security.

Fig 7.1
Skipton, Yorkshire 1933. Riveted high-pressure bullet tank.
[© IGEM]

Fig 7.2
Skipton, Yorkshire, 1933. A close-up of the Skipton high-pressure bullet tank, with a man standing alongside for scale.
[© IGEM]

Fig 7.3
Canvey Island, Essex, 1936. The Hortonsphere.
[© IGEM]

Fig 7.4
Canvey Island, Essex, c 1950. The Onion and Sausage, high-pressure gasholders.
[© IGEM]

Fig 7.5
Rayleigh, Essex, 1939. Riveted high-pressure bullet tank.
[© IGEM]

Fig 7.6
Oakengates, Shropshire, 1940. Riveted high-pressure bullet tanks.
[© NGA]

Fig 7.7
Shanklin, Isle of Wight, 1950. Welded high-pressure bullet tank.
[© IGEM]

Fig 7.8
Abingdon, Oxfordshire, 1968. Half of a bullet tank section travelling through Abingdon.
[© IGEM]

Fig 7.9
Abingdon, Oxfordshire 1968. Rotating the bullet tank sections into position.
[© IGEM]

Fig 7.10
Abingdon, Oxfordshire, 1968. Welding the two sections of the bullet tank together at the site.
[© IGEM]

7 HIGH-PRESSURE GASHOLDERS

Fig 7.11
Cowley, Oxfordshire, 1968. High-pressure bullet tanks.
[© IGEM]

Fig 7.12
Isle of Grain, Kent, c 1960. High-pressure bullet tanks.
[© NGA]

7 HIGH-PRESSURE GASHOLDERS

Fig 7.13
Biggin Hill, London, 2018. The pipe array high-pressure storage site.
[© Keith Ellison]

Fig 7.14
Poole, Dorset, 1966. Construction of a Hortonsphere for butane storage.
[© IGEM]

Fig 7.15
Bicester, Oxfordshire, 1967. Construction of two Hortonspheres for LPG storage at the new gasworks.
[© IGEM]

Fig 7.16
Hilsea, Portsmouth, 1967. Testing of the emergency water spray system on the Hortonspheres used for LPG storage.
[© IGEM]

Fig 7.17
Canvey Island, Essex, 2005. The gas terminal.
[© Historic England Archive 24072/033]

Fig 7.18
Isle of Grain, Kent, 1980. One of the LNG tanks at the gas storage site.
[© IGEM]

Fig 7.19
Isle of Grain, Kent, 2023. LNG import terminal from above.
[© National Grid Grain LNG]

7 HIGH-PRESSURE GASHOLDERS

8 Gasholder construction

The construction of gasholders was a challenging activity requiring a high degree of accuracy, and the equipment available was quite simple by modern standards. The construction of the water tank was the first task; it could be built above or below ground. Above-ground tanks were first constructed from wood but were soon replaced by cast iron such as that which survives at Lavenham (Fig 8.1). These tanks were superseded by steel tanks, at first riveted and later welded construction as shown in Figs 8.2 and 8.3. The construction of waterless and high-pressure gasholders is considered in their respective chapters.

The preference, where the ground conditions allowed, was to construct the tank below ground from stone or brick, and waterproof this with an outer layer of puddle clay. This required a lot of excavation as seen in Fig 8.4.

Concrete was used in tank construction from 1870; it could be waterproofed by a layer of render on the inside wall of the tank. One of the earliest examples is shown in Fig 8.5.

A concrete gasholder tank from 1950 can be seen in Fig 8.6, the tank walls and mound in the centre of the tank known as a dumpling. Concrete reinforced by steel was also used to build gasholder tanks (Fig 8.7).

The construction of gasholders was a massive feat, often using only simple cranes as seen in Figs 8.2 and 8.8 and large amounts of manual labour.

The metal components were preconstructed in sections at the factory. This included the bending and cutting of girders and sheeting to the precise size. They were then taken to site and assembled. Typically, the largest (outer) lift would be built first and then the engineers would work inwards as seen in Fig 8.9. The metal components would be riveted (Fig 8.10) or welded together (*see* Fig 8.18) to construct the tank and gasholder.

Once the lifts had been installed, the innermost lift would require the construction of a domed roof called a crown to hold in the gas. The crown, which was constructed of metal sheeting, could be supported by internal trusses, shown being installed in Fig 8.11, or untrussed. The untrussed crown would keep its shape when filled with gas; however, it needed a structure called a crown rest (Fig 8.12) to support the crown when the gasholder was empty of gas.

The cast iron columns used to support gasholders were built in sections and bolted together internally so the joins were not visible when painted. The columns were lifted into place and connected to one another by one or more tiers of horizontal girders (Fig 8.13). Frame-guided gasholders were constructed from sections of steel riveted together, providing a strong but light frame (Fig 8.14).

Space was always at a premium on gasworks, which led to some gasholders sharing a column, as was the case with gasholders No 4 and No 5 at the Kennington Oval, London, shown in Fig 8.15.

Old gasholders were often rebuilt as spiral-guided gasholders, as was the case of this example built at Linacre gasworks in Bootle, Liverpool (Figs 8.16 and 8.17), the lifts being built from the inner lift outwards. As each ring of panels for the lift was riveted together, it was lowered into the tank, with the next ring of panels then being added until the lift reached the base of the tank.

Gasholders required maintenance and repair, such as patch welding (Fig 8.18), especially during wartime. Sludge and debris would build up in the tank, which would require removal, sometimes requiring a diver to enter the tank as shown in Fig 8.19. Gasholders required painting on a regular basis to ensure the tank and lifts did not corrode as seen in Fig 8.20. If they did corrode, then they would need resheeting as shown in Fig 8.21.

Fig 8.1
Lavenham, Suffolk, 2023. The restored single-lift column gasholder with a cast iron tank.
[© Jam Butty Photography and Video and IPB Communications]

Fig 8.2
Basingstoke, Hampshire, 1958. Construction of a riveted steel tank at the gasworks.
[© IGEM]

Fig 8.3
Saltash, Cornwall, 1949. Construction of a gasholder with a steel tank, using a hand crane.
[© IGEM]

Fig 8.4
Beckton, London, 1869. Construction of No 3 gasholder.
[© IGEM]

Fig 8.5
Old Kent Road, London, 1890. Construction of the concrete tank for No 13 gasholder.
[© NGA]

Fig 8.6
Woodford, London, 1950. Completed concrete gasholder tank.
[© IGEM]

Fig 8.7
Deal, Kent, 1962. Construction of a reinforced concrete gasholder tank.
[© IGEM]

Fig 8.8
Cannon Lane, Pinner, London, 1957. A Scotch derrick being used in the construction of a spiral-guided gasholder.
[© IGEM]

Fig 8.9
Basingstoke, Hampshire, 1958. Construction of a spiral-guided gasholder: installing the sheeting within the lift wall.
[© IGEM]

Fig 8.10
Crawley, West Sussex, c 1958. Riveting on the construction of a spiral-guided gasholder.
[© NGA]

Fig 8.11
Beckton, London, 1945. Reconstruction of No 2 gasholder as a spiral-guided gasholder.
[© IGEM]

Fig 8.12
Keyham, Plymouth, 1951. Repairing the crown sheeting on an untrussed gasholder with the wooden crown rest revealed.
[© IGEM]

Fig 8.13
Lymm, Cheshire, c 1880. Construction of a column-guided gasholder by W C Holmes Engineers.
[© IGEM]

8 GASHOLDER CONSTRUCTION

Fig 8.15
Kennington, London, 2017. The conjoined No 4 and No 5 gasholders at the Oval.
[© Historic England Archive DP182540]

Fig 8.14
Bradford Road, Manchester, 2023. Detail of the riveting on the gasholder.
[© Jam Butty Photography and Video and IPB Communications]

Fig 8.16
Bootle, Liverpool, c 1950. Conversion of gasholder No 8 to a spiral-guided gasholder, construction of outer lift.
[© NGA]

Fig 8.17
Bootle, Liverpool, c 1950. Painting spiral-guided gasholder No 8.
[© NGA]

Fig 8.18
Beckton, London, 1937. Patch welding gasholder No 1.
[© IGEM]

Fig 8.19
Beckton, London, 1937. Diver descending into the tank of gasholder No 5.
[© IGEM]

Fig 8.20
Pickering, Yorkshire, 1958. Flame cleaning and repainting of a two-lift column-guided gasholder.
[© IGEM]

Fig 8.21
Castleford, Yorkshire, 1928. Resheeting of the gasholder.
[© IGEM]

9 Gasholders on the landscape

The variety of locations and landscapes in which gasholders could be found was vast, with over 3,600 former gasworks and gasholder sites known to have existed in England. Despite the expectation that gasworks were to be found in heavily industrialised urban areas, many were found in more rural settings, such as those shown in Figs 9.1–9.6.

Transporting coal was one of the biggest costs associated with gas production. Being located on the coast was a great benefit to gasworks, especially if they had an adjacent quay, as it allowed coal to be transported directly to the gasworks by colliers (Figs 9.7–9.13). These were special ships which plied their trade taking coal from the coal fields of north-east England to ports along the coast of England.

Gasworks were also located in provincial towns and cities (Figs 9.14–9.18). These could be set against historic city skylines (Fig 9.17) or as an integral part of the industrial landscape (Fig 9.19). Gasworks were typically located next to rivers and had access to railways for easy access to coal, often supplied by the coal fields of the Midlands and the north of England. As town gas was lighter than air, the location of the gasworks and gasholders at a low altitude was an important factor.

London had the highest concentration of gasworks in the United Kingdom (Figs 9.19–9.23). The Poplar gasholders and East Greenwich No 1 gasholder (Fig 9.21) have now been demolished, but the column- and frame-guided gasholders at Bethnal Green (Fig 9.22) and the column-guided gasholders at Bromley-by-Bow (Fig 9.20) are to be incorporated into new developments.

Fig 9.1
Rayleigh, Essex, 1912. A typical small gasworks, with the shop and offices on the road frontage and a small column-guided gasholder in a steel tank visible to the rear.
[© IGEM]

Fig 9.2
Amersham, Buckinghamshire, 1913. The gasworks was on the edge of the town and surrounded by fields. A column-guided gasholder in a cast iron tank and a frame-guided gasholder in a steel tank are visible.
[© IGEM]

Fig 9.3
Ascot, Surrey, 1949. These rural gasworks also supplied electricity. Two spiral-guided and one frame-guided gasholder in steel tanks are visible.
[© IGEM]

GASHOLDERS: A HISTORY IN PICTURES

9 GASHOLDERS ON THE LANDSCAPE

Fig 9.5
Grange-over-Sands, Cumbria, c 1970. A two-lift spiral-guided gasholder visible at the gasworks, which was one of the last to close in England.
[© NGA]

Fig 9.4
Brierfield, Lancashire, 2023. The gasholder is set in open countryside adjacent to the mill it originally supplied when part of the Brierfield gasworks.
[© Jam Butty Photography and Video and IPB Communications]

Fig 9.6
Cookham, Berkshire, 1996. This site was never a gasworks but was built as a site to store gas.
[© IGEM]

Fig 9.7
Minehead, Somerset, 1930. The gasworks were located on the seafront, with a single frame-guided gasholder visible.
[© Historic England Archive EPW033301]

9 GASHOLDERS ON THE LANDSCAPE

Fig 9.8
Torquay, Devon, c 1945. The gasworks was still camouflaged following the Second World War, with four frame-guided gasholders visible. It was one of 16 gasworks which produced hydrogen gas for barrage balloons during the war.
[© NGA]

9 GASHOLDERS ON THE LANDSCAPE

Fig 9.9
Whitby, Yorkshire, 1959. Set on the banks of the River Esk. It was the first town in England to have natural gas supplied from an onshore gas field; the gas was converted to town gas before use.
[© IGEM]

GASHOLDERS: A HISTORY IN PICTURES

9 GASHOLDERS ON THE LANDSCAPE

Fig 9.10
Beckton, London, c 1970. Once the largest gasworks in the world, shown here with the coking works and pier which had been used to import coal.
[© NGA]

Fig 9.11
Falmouth, Cornwall, c 1949. Its cramped location required the gasworks to expand into the harbour.
[© NGA]

Fig 9.12
Poole, Dorset, 1949. The gasworks were built on land reclaimed from Poole Harbour.
[© IGEM]

9 GASHOLDERS ON THE LANDSCAPE

Fig 9.13
Haven Road, Exeter, c 1949. These gasworks were built alongside the Exeter Ship Canal, with access to coal delivered by sea.
[© IGEM]

Fig 9.14
Kidderminster, Worcestershire, c 1950. Located between the River Stour and the Staffordshire and Worcestershire Canal, the large MAN gasholder was a feature of the gasworks.
[© NGA]

Fig 9.15
Huddersfield, Yorkshire, 1965. A view from a train window, with the gasworks visible in the distance.
[© Historic England Archive AA083934]

Fig 9.16
Aylestone Road, Leicester, 1931. This former gasworks is today the home of the National Gas Museum.
[© Historic England Archive EPW035989]

9 GASHOLDERS ON THE LANDSCAPE

Fig 9.17
York, 1924. View from the gasworks across York to the Minster.
[© NGA]

Fig 9.18
Reading, Berkshire, 1932. An aerial view of the gasworks on the banks of the River Kennet, with the River Thames in the background.
[© Historic England Archive EPW037494]

GASHOLDERS: A HISTORY IN PICTURES

9 GASHOLDERS ON THE LANDSCAPE

Fig 9.19
Bromley-by-Bow, London, c 1970. Bromley-by-Bow gasworks (front), West Ham Power Station (rear left) and Poplar gasholders (rear right) across the River Lea.
[© IGEM]

Fig 9.20
Bromley-by-Bow, London, 2021. The gasholders with Canary Wharf behind.
[© Historic England Archive DP413990]

GASHOLDERS: A HISTORY IN PICTURES

9 GASHOLDERS ON THE LANDSCAPE

Fig 9.22
Bethnal Green, London, 2021. View of the gasholders from across the Regent's Canal.
[© Historic England Archive DP434053]

Fig 9.21
East Greenwich, London, 2017. Gasholder No 1 with the Millennium Dome behind.
[© Historic England Archive DP182577]

Fig 9.23
Battersea, London, 2012. View of the MAN gasholder and Battersea Power Station.
[© Historic England Archive DP148851]

10 Gasholders and society

Gasworks were focal points in the communities they served, with gasholders making prominent features on the skyline (Fig 10.1). Staff from the gas company (Fig 10.2) would be a familiar sight, installing new appliances, repairing gas mains, or reading gas meters. Gasholders found use for advertising, in the case of Stone gasworks (Fig 10.3), for the local brewery.

The iconic nature of gasholders attracted the attention of artists. The artwork produced by Cyril Farey of Beckton gasworks (Fig 10.4) was used in promotional material by the GLCC.

Large gasworks, like the Bradford Road gasworks in Manchester (Fig 10.5), formed the centre of large urban communities. These gasworks were operated by the Manchester Corporation, who had controlled Manchester's gas supply since the Manchester Police had established it in 1817.

Until their dismantling, the colossal Bradford Road gasholders had provided a backdrop to the area since 1894 (Fig 10.6).

To boost supply, Manchester built a new gasworks 10 miles south of the city in Partington. The importance of the gas industry was recognised by regular royal visits, including that of the Duke of Edinburgh to Partington gasworks in 1955 (Fig 10.7).

Gasworks required good transport links, such as railways or canals (Fig 10.8) to import coal. They were often located adjacent to this infrastructure. Otherwise, the coal would have to be transported to the gasworks by road, using a horse and cart (Fig 10.9) or lorry.

The gritty urban sites, often in neglected parts of the city (Fig 10.10), have gradually been brought back into use. An example which has reused the gasholders is the Kings Cross development (Fig 10.11).

The gas industry played a significant role in the First and Second World Wars, providing fuel for industry and many important by-products used in everything from explosives to medicines. During the Second World War, gasworks were targeted by the German air force, due to their strategic importance in the war effort (Figs 10.12 and 10.13). Often, only the heroic actions of staff saved the gasworks from destruction during air raids, cutting off the gas supplies to damaged gasholders and plant.

As staff signed up for military service, shortages of labour occurred. Women were brought in to undertake many of the roles previously performed by men in the gas industry (Figs 10.14–10.16).

A gas lamp burns at the memorial garden on the former Bromley-by-Bow gasworks; with it are the memorials to the many gas workers who lost their lives during both world wars (Fig 10.17).

The modern developments of Canary Wharf are in stark contrast to the classically designed gasholders of Bromley-by-Bow (Fig 10.18).

Larger gas undertakings had associated sports clubs and recreation grounds, often overlooked by the gasholders (Fig 10.19). The Bristol Rovers Football Club, who had their old Eastville stadium adjacent to the Stapleton Road gasworks (Fig 10.20), were affectionately known as 'The Gas'.

Probably the best-known gasholder in the world is gasholder No 1 at the Oval, forming the backdrop of many famous cricket matches (Fig 10.21). The archivist of the Oval Cricket Ground, Bill Gordon, is pictured in Fig 10.22.

Fig 10.1
Blackburn, Lancashire, c 1970. A frame-guided gasholder on the skyline.
[© NGA]

Fig 10.2
Bournemouth, Dorset, 1953. Southern Gas Board fitter by his Austin A40 van at the gasworks.
[© IGEM]

10 GASHOLDERS AND SOCIETY

Fig 10.3
Stone, Staffordshire, 1933. The Stone Gas and Electricity Company Works from the air.
[© Historic England Archive EPW042626]

GASHOLDERS: A HISTORY IN PICTURES

Fig 10.4
Beckton gasworks, London, 1930. A view across gasworks by Cyril Farey.
[© IGEM]

10 GASHOLDERS AND SOCIETY

Fig 10.5
Bradford Road, Manchester, 1965. A view across the gasworks.
[© NGA]

Fig 10.6
Bradford Road, Manchester, 2016.
[© Historic England Archive DP186283]

Fig 10.7
Partington, Manchester, 1955. The Duke of Edinburgh in his Land Rover visiting the gasworks.
[© NGA]

GASHOLDERS: A HISTORY IN PICTURES

Fig 10.8
Lytton Street, Stoke on Trent, 1968. Moored canal boats in front of a spiral-guided gasholder.
[© Historic England Archive DES01/04/0467]

Fig 10.9
Kings Cross, London, c 1950. Horse and cart in front of the gasholders.
[© Historic England Archive AA065988]

Fig 10.10
Kings Cross, London, c 1950. Traffic passing behind a gas lamp, with the gasholders in the background.
[© Historic England Archive AA066009]

Fig 10.11
Kings Cross, London 2017. The gasholder redevelopment, with flats built within the gasholder triplet and a public park within the former gasholder No 8.
[© Historic England DP220098]

Fig 10.12
Beckton, London, 1940. Gasholder No 2 following a bombing raid.
[© IGEM]

Fig 10.13
Beckton, London, 1942. Gasholder No 2 on fire.
[© IGEM]

Fig 10.14
Bromley-by-Bow, London, 1917. Women chipping and painting a gasholder.
[© IGEM]

10 GASHOLDERS AND SOCIETY

Fig 10.15
Hilsea, Portsmouth, 1919. Women workers, war staff in front of gasholder.
[© IGEM]

Fig 10.16
Beckton, London, 1942. Women scraping and painting gasholder No 4.
[© IGEM]

Fig 10.17
Bromley-by-Bow, London 2021. The memorial garden with the gas lamps burning and a gasholder behind.
[© Historic England DP413983]

10 GASHOLDERS AND SOCIETY

GASHOLDERS: A HISTORY IN PICTURES

Fig 10.18
Bromley-by-Bow, London, 2021. The gasholders
juxtaposed against the Canary Wharf development.
[© Historic England DP413996]

10 GASHOLDERS AND SOCIETY

Fig 10.19
Alder Road, Bournemouth, 1950. Bowls being played at the Southern Gas Board's sports ground, with gasholders in the background.
[© IGEM]

GASHOLDERS: A HISTORY IN PICTURES

10 GASHOLDERS AND SOCIETY

Fig 10.21
Kennington, London, c 1950. Gasholder No 1 as a backdrop to a cricket match at the Oval.
[© NGA]

Fig 10.20
Stapleton Road, Bristol, 1926. The gasworks adjacent to the Bristol Rovers Eastville stadium.
[© Historic England Archive EPW016974]

Fig 10.22
Kennington, London, 2016. Bill Gordon, the archivist and pavilion curator at the Oval Cricket Ground.
[© Historic England]

11 Gasholder engineers and manufacturers

The gas industry was dependent for success on the quality of its engineers and the companies which manufactured their equipment. There were many great engineers, some of whom have already been discussed, and many great companies could be included in this chapter, but we have provided just a few examples.

Thomas Hawksley (see Fig 11.3) practised throughout his professional career in water and gas engineering. He was a member of the Royal Society and was a president of the British Association of Gas Managers, the Institution of Civil Engineers and the Institution of Mechanical Engineers.

In 1860 a new gasworks was built for the Sunderland Gas Company at Hendon. It was designed by Hawksley's company T and C Hawksley, and included a column-guided gasholder whose frame survives today and is Grade II listed (Fig 11.1).

One of the quirkier surviving gasholders is the Gothic-styled Grade II listed gasholder designed by Robert Paulson Spice (see Fig 11.3) at Great Yarmouth (Fig 11.2). The Norwich-born Spice was an articled apprentice to a blacksmith in Fakenham, the home of England's last surviving gasworks, which Spice originally built. He went on to design many gasworks, including Great Yarmouth and Tunbridge Wells. He was a president of the Gas Institute and a notable travel writer.

Charles Hunt (see Fig 11.3) was born in Great Yarmouth. He originally worked for the City of London GLCC. He joined the Birmingham GLCC as chief engineer at the age of 30 in 1872. The company was purchased by the Birmingham Corporation in 1875 and Hunt was given the job of redesigning the Windsor Street gasworks, which included the construction of the two largest gasholders (6.5 million ft^3) in the world at that time (Figs 11.4 and 11.5).

Two great engineers were responsible for the design of the gasholders at Kensal Green (Figs 11.6–11.9): Vitruvius Wyatt, who designed the smaller gasholder No 5, and George Trewby, who designed the larger gasholder No 6, affectionately known as 'The Colonel'. Trewby is pictured in the centre of Fig 11.6 along with Samuel Cutler whose company built The Colonel.

Samuel Cutler and Sons went on to develop a gasholder design with a geodesic cylindrical frame known as the Cutler patent guide frame. This strong and relatively light design was exported all over the world (Figs 11.10–11.12).

Thomas Newbigging (see Fig 11.15) was a renowned author, poet and president of the Institution of Gas Engineers; he became manager of the Rossendale Union Gas Company, Lancashire, in 1857. In 1870 he moved to Brazil to become manager of Pernambuco gasworks before establishing a consulting practice in Manchester in 1875. His son John became engineer of the Manchester Corporation Gas Department in 1900 and was involved in the design of gasholders built at the Bradford Road Gasworks, Manchester (Fig 11.13), by Ashmore, Benson, Pease and Co Ltd (Fig 11.14).

The Livesey family's involvement goes back to the early years of the GLCC. Most notable among them were George Livesey (Fig 11.15) and his brother Frank, who worked for the South Metropolitan Gas Company, who were responsible for some of the most iconic frame-guided gasholders built. The Livesey family had strong links with the South London communities in which they lived, and were strong proponents of the co-partnership schemes, which gave employees a profit share in the companies in which they worked.

George Livesey's most notable gasholders were the listed gasholder No 13 built at Old Kent Road, London (Figs 11.16 and 11.17) and gasholders No 1 (Fig 11.18) and No 2 (Fig 11.19) built at East Greenwich by Ashmore, Benson, Pease and Co Ltd and Clayton, Son and Co Ltd, respectively. The Clayton, Son and Co Ltd construction gang features in Fig 11.20.

Fig 11.1
Hendon, Sunderland, 2008. Hawksley's gasholder.
[© Historic England Archive DP033968]

Fig 11.2
Great Yarmouth, 2000. Robert Spice's gasholder.
[© Mike Glyde]

11 GASHOLDER ENGINEERS AND MANUFACTURERS

Fig 11.3
L–R: Thomas Hawksley, Robert Paulson Spice and Charles Hunt.
[© IGEM]

11 GASHOLDER ENGINEERS AND MANUFACTURERS

Fig 11.4
Windsor Street, Birmingham, 1971. Charles Hunt's giant twin frame-guided gasholders.
[© IGEM]

Fig 11.5
Windsor Street, Birmingham, 2015.
[© Historic England Archive 29418/054]

GASHOLDERS: A HISTORY IN PICTURES

Fig 11.6
Kensal Green, London. 1911. The inauguration of gasholder No 6.
[© IGEM]

Fig 11.7
Kensal Green, London, 2016. Gasholders No 5 and No 6 from the Kensal Green cemetery.
[© Historic England Archive DP183491]

11 GASHOLDER ENGINEERS AND MANUFACTURERS

Fig 11.8
Kensal Green, London, 2016. Close-up of the framing of gasholder No 6.
[© Historic England Archive DP183494]

Fig 11.9
Kensal Green, London, 2019. Gasholders No 5 and No 6.
[© AtkinsRéalis]

11 GASHOLDER ENGINEERS AND MANUFACTURERS

Fig 11.10
Advertisement for Samuel Cutler and Sons patent guide-frame gasholder, 1901.
[© IGEM]

Fig 11.11
New Barnet, London, 2018. Cutler patent guide-frame gasholder.
[© Rebecca Delaney]

Fig 11.12
Hornsey, London, 2016. Cutler patent guide-frame gasholder, 2016.
[© Rebecca Delaney]

Fig 11.13
Bradford Road, Manchester, 2016.
[© Historic England Archive DP186279]

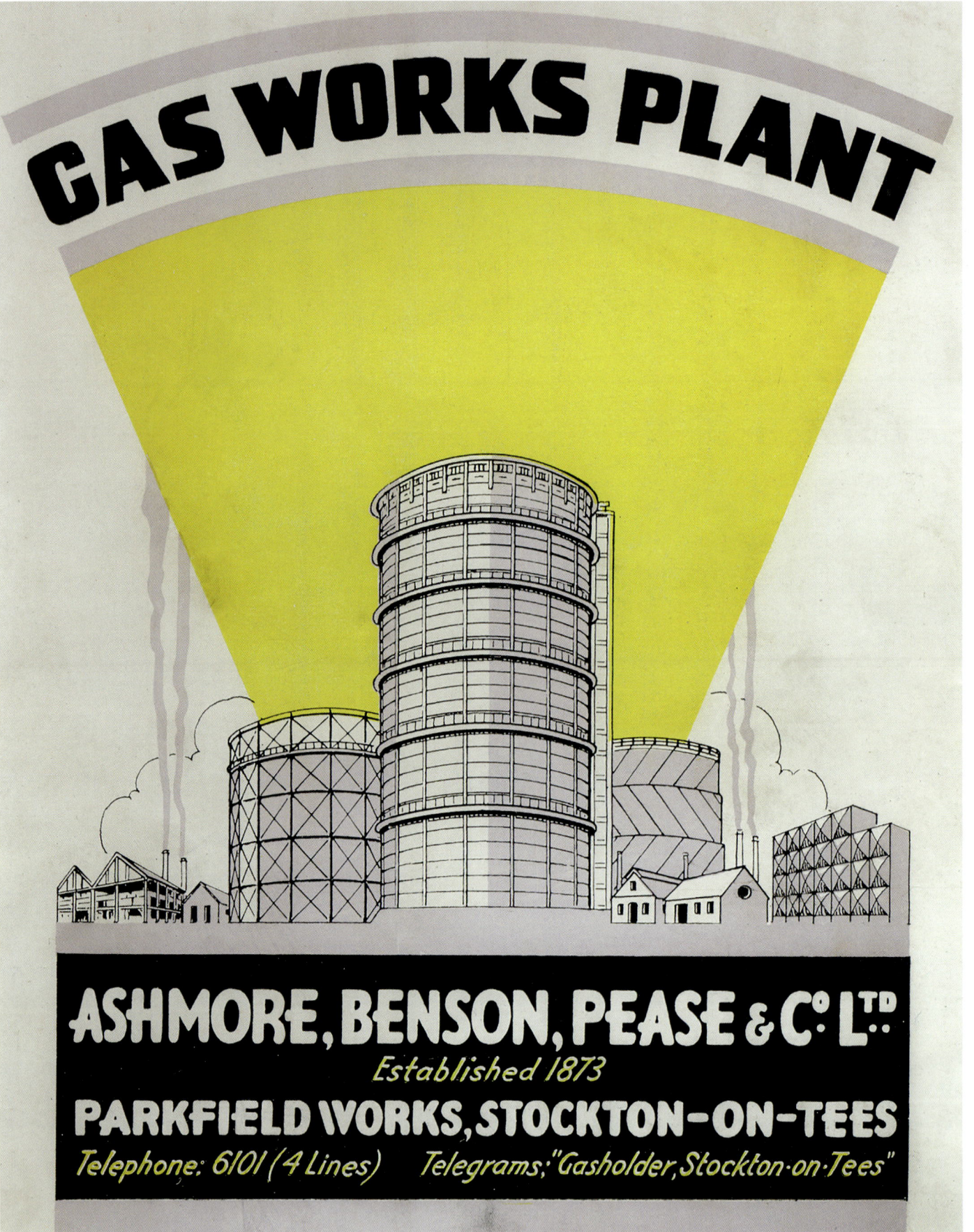

Fig 11.14
Ashmore, Benson, Pease and Co Ltd catalogue, 1930.
[IGEM]

Fig 11.15
Thomas Newbigging (left) and George Livesey (right).
[IGEM]

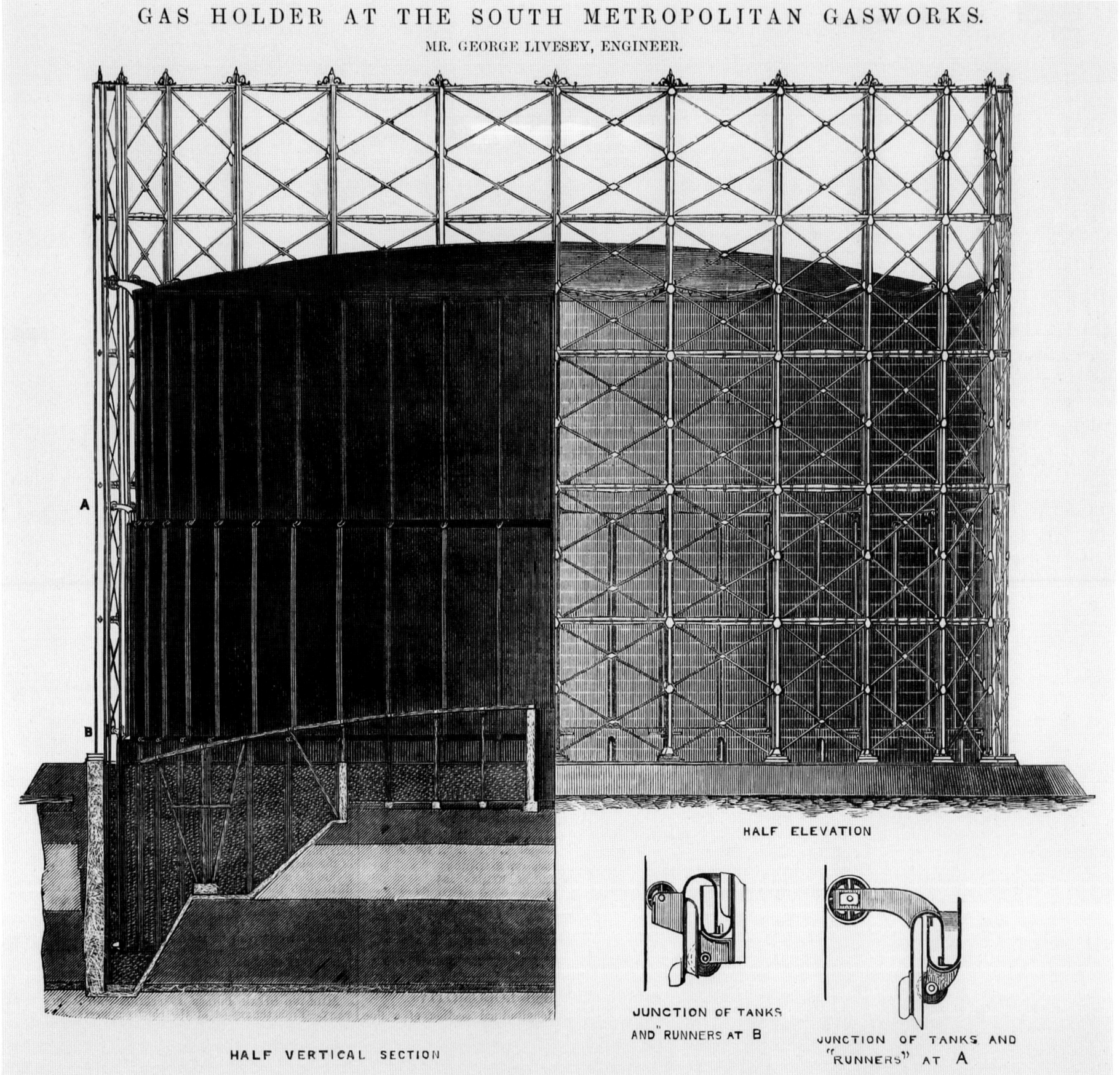

11 GASHOLDER ENGINEERS AND MANUFACTURERS

Fig 11.17
Old Kent Road, London, 2017. The listed gasholder No 13.
[© Historic England Archive 33085/017]

Fig 11.16
Old Kent Road, London, 1881. George Livesey's drawing of gasholder No 13.
[IGEM]

GASHOLDERS: A HISTORY IN PICTURES

Fig 11.18
East Greenwich, London, 2017. Gasholder No 1.
[© Historic England Archive DP182573]

Fig 11.19
Advertisement for Clayton, Son and Co Ltd, 1901, featuring East Greenwich gasholder No 2.
[IGEM]

Fig 11.20
The Clayton, Son and Co Ltd, 1930. Gasholder construction gang.
[IGEM]

12 The future

Once vital, gasholders have now become redundant, disappearing relics of our industrial heritage.

While some observers may lament the loss of these often imposing structures, dismantling has always been part of the industrial story. Many gasholders were replaced due to obsolescence or insufficient capacity for local needs. Others were re-erected in new locations, or the tanks were repurposed for storing materials.

This chapter captures some of the vast changes in the landscape before and after the gasholders were replaced. The significance of many of these sites has been documented through photography, exhibitions, education and repurposing of historical materials.

For those gasholders that have a particular significance, there is a story of rebirth and revival as part of a post-industrial reimagining. For example, the oldest gasholder in the world at Fulham, London, is finding a new purpose as part of the wider residential-led development by St William (part of the Berkeley Group), known as King's Road Park. It is envisaged it will be transformed as part of a new public park anchored in the legacy of gas heritage.

Projects with the ambition of King's Road Park unfold with considerable complexity, requiring specialist contractors to navigate the intricate process of dismantling the cast iron frames, refurbishing in bespoke workshops, and then re-erection on site. St William's development in Bethnal Green, London, weaves the two Victorian gasholders into the modern and vibrant fabric of today in a spectacular canal-side redevelopment. In some cases, parts of the gasholder have been retained for use as part of the redevelopment to commemorate and celebrate the gas heritage, for example at sites like Poplar and Battersea in London by St William.

From these projects and many others, the legacy of the gas industry, marked by the rise and fall of gasholders, is not confined to the pages of history. It thrives in the presence of the reimagined structures in our urban landscapes. Gasholders, once silent giants, now echo a narrative of resilience, adaptation and the enduring spirit of progress – their legacy lives on, not just in the remnants of the dismantled structures but in the sustainable communities that rise in their stead.

Fig 12.1
Oxford, 1956. Dismantling of gasholder No 1.
[© IGEM]

Fig 12.2
Fulham, London, 1951. Dismantling of gasholder No 5.
[© IGEM]

GASHOLDERS: A HISTORY IN PICTURES

Fig 12.3
Kings Cross, London, 2009. The dismantled triplet gasholders placed in special protective casings stored around gasholder No 8, still standing.
[© Historic England Archive 26448/019]

12 THE FUTURE

Fig 12.4
Kings Cross, London, 2017. Gasholder Park.
[© Historic England Archive DP220106]

Fig 12.5
Kings Cross, London, 2018. The central atrium of the apartments built within the redeveloped gasholder triplet.
[© Historic England Archive DP221352]

12 THE FUTURE

Fig 12.6
Fulham, London, 1949. Gasholder No 2 while still in operation.
[© IGEM]

Fig 12.7
Fulham, London, 1954. Former gasworks site.
[© IGEM]

Fig 12.8
Fulham, London. Artistic impression of the future redevelopment of the area, submitted as part of the planning application.
[© St William]

Fig 12.9
Fulham, London. An indicative image of what the future redevelopment of the site could look like.
[© St William]

GASHOLDERS: A HISTORY IN PICTURES

12 THE FUTURE

Fig 12.10
Canon's Marsh, Bristol, 1954.
[© Historic England Archive EAW000699]

Fig 12.11
Canon's Marsh, Bristol, 2024. The shells of the former retort and purifier houses which survived were redeveloped into residential properties along the waterfront.
[© Jam Butty Photography and Video and IPB Communications]

Fig 12.13
Battersea, London, 2024. Incorporation of the former gasholder frame into the Battersea redevelopment.
[© St William]

Fig 12.12
Battersea, London, 1954.
[© IGEM]

Fig 12.14
Kennington, London, 2021. Dismantling of gasholders No 4 and No 5, Kennington Oval.
[© Historic England Archive DP413880]

12 THE FUTURE

Fig 12.15
Kennington, London, 2023. Redevelopment of the site in progress.
[© Berkeley Group]

Fig 12.16
Kennington, London. Artistic impression of the future redevelopment.
[© Berkeley Group]

Fig 12.17
Kennington, London. Artistic impression of the future redevelopment.
[© Berkeley Group]

12 THE FUTURE

Fig 12.19
Bethnal Green, London. Rendered images of the proposed redevelopment.
[© St William]

Fig 12.18
Bethnal Green, London, 2021.
[© Phil Edwards]

Fig 12.20
Bromley-by-Bow, London, c 1970.
[© IGEM]

Fig 12.21
Bromley-by-Bow, London. Artistic impression of the proposed redevelopment of the area.
[© St William]

Further resources

Fakenham Gasworks Museum: https://fakenhamgasmuseum.com/
Historic England Manufactured Gas resources: https://historicengland.org.uk/research/current/discover-and-understand/industry-and-infrastructure/manufactured-gas-industry/
Institution of Gas Engineers and Managers, History Panel: www.igem.org.uk/news-and-media/historic-gas-times.html
National Gas Archive: https://extranet.nationalgrid.com/GasArchive/
National Gas Museum: www.nationalgasmuseum.org.uk/

References

Berger, B 2019 *Der Gasbehälter als Bautypus*. Munich: TUM-University Press
Historic England 2019 *Gasworks and Redundant Gasholders: Guidelines for their Evaluation and Recording*. Swindon: Historic England
Historic England 2020 *Gasworks and Gasholders: Introductions to Heritage Assets*, HEAG296. Swindon: Historic England
Thomas, R 2020 *The Manufactured Gas Industry*, Vols 1–5, Research Report Series no 182-2020. Swindon: Historic England
Tucker, M 2000 *The Development of the Gasholder in London in the Later Nineteenth Century*. London: English Heritage

Index

Page numbers in **bold** refer to figures

Abingdon, Oxfordshire 111, **116**, **117**, **118**
above-ground tanks 15, 79, 128
Accum, Christian, *Practical Treatise on Gas Light* 15, **17**
advertisements 79, 80, **94**, 165, **167**, **196**, **205**
Alder Road, Bournemouth **183**
Aldershot, Hampshire **76**
Alresford, Hampshire 1, **6**
Amersham, Buckinghamshire **145**
artworks 165, **168**
Ascot, Surrey **145**
Ashmore, Benson, Pease and Co Ltd 98, 187, **200**
Augsburg Gasworks, Germany 98
Aylestone Road, Leicester **158**

Basingstoke, Hampshire **130**, **135**
Bath 1, **10**, **75**
Battersea, London 15, **32**, 98, **99**, **100**, **164**, 206, **216**, **217**
Beckton, London 1, **4**, **12**, 15, **142**, **152**, 165, **168**
   column-guided gasholders **31**, 35, **40**
   construction **130**, **137**
   frame-guided gasholders **31**, 56, **57**
   Second World War **176**, **177**, **180**
   spiral-guided gasholders **6**, **31**, **81**, **137**
below-ground tanks 79, 80, **196**, **205**
Berkshire
   Cookham **148**
   Reading **64**, **159**
   Windsor 1, **11**
Bethnal Green, London 15, **27**, 56, 144, **163**, 206, **222**, **223**
Bicester, Oxfordshire **123**
Biggin Hill, London 111, **121**
Birkshall, Bradford **94**
Birmingham, Windsor Street 187, **190**, **191**
Birmingham Corporation Gas Department 98, 187
Bishop Auckland, County Durham **85**
Bishop Bridge Road, Norwich **86**
Blackburn, Lancashire **28**, 165
Blackfriars, London 35, **47**
Blakeney, Gloucestershire 1, **6**
Bootle, Liverpool 35, **44**, **45**, 128, **140**, **141**
Boston, Lincolnshire **83**
Boulton and Watt 1, 15
Bourne Valley, Poole, Dorset **63**
Bournemouth, Dorset **166**
   Alder Road **183**
Bow Common, London 35, **41**
bracing 15, 35, 56
Bradford, Birkshall **94**
Bradford Road, Manchester **65**, **66**, **139**, 165, **169**, **170**, 187, **199**
Brierfield, Lancashire **146**
Bristol
   Canon's Marsh **214**, **215**
   Stapleton Road **184**

Bristol Rovers Football Club 165, **184**
Bromley-by-Bow, London 35, **51**, **52**, **53**, 144, **160**, **161**, 165, **178**, **181**, **182**, **224**, **225**
Buckinghamshire, Amersham **145**
buttressing 56

Cadwell Lane, Hitchin 1
camouflage **150**
Cannon Lane, Pinner, London **134**
Cannon Street, Middlesbrough **94**
Canon's Marsh, Bristol **214**, **215**
Canvey Island Liquefied Natural Gas (LNG) Terminal, Essex 98, **110**, 111, **112**, **113**, **125**
capacity 15, 79, 206
Carlisle 35, **49**
cast iron 15, **22**, 35, **40**, 56, **57**, **58**, 128, **129**, 145, 206
Castleford, Yorkshire **143**
Cheshire
   Lymm **138**
   Northwich 79
Chicago Bridge & Iron Company 111
City of London GLCC 35, 187
Clayton, Son and Co Ltd **107**, 187, **205**
Clegg, Samuel 1, 15, **15**, 98
Cloughfold, Lancashire **2**
coal 1, **5**, **13**, 15, 144, **152**, **155**, 165
coke ovens 1, **12**, 152
colour schemes 79, **87**, **150**
column-guided gasholders 35
   Amersham **145**
   Battersea **32**
   Beckton **31**, 35, **40**
   Blackfriars, London 35, **47**
   Bootle 35, **44**, **45**
   Bow Common **41**
   Bromley-by-Bow 35, **51**, **52**, **53**, 144, 160, 161, 178, 181, 182
   Carlisle 35, **49**
   construction **138**
   decorative features 35, **38**, **39**, **40**, **41**, **43**, **52**, **53**
   Fulham **34**, 35, **38**, **39**
   Gunnislake **36**
   Hendon 187, **187**
   Kennington Oval 35, **42**, **43**
   Kings Cross **54**, **55**, **173**, **174**, **175**, 208, **209**, **210**
   Lymm **138**
   Oxford **20**, 206
   Pickering **143**
   Portsmouth 35, **50**
   Preston **37**
   redevelopment 35, **175**, 206, **223**, **225**
   Ryde **30**
   Salford 35, **48**
   Scarborough 35, **46**
   single-lift **22**, **36**, **129**

   South Shields **25**
   three-lift 35, **47**
   two-lift 35, **44**, **45**, **46**, **143**
concrete 98, 128, **131**, **132**, **133**
condensers 1, **6**, **7**
construction 128
   Basingstoke **130**, **135**
   Beckton **130**, **137**
   Bootle **140**, **141**
   Cannon Lane, Pinner **134**
   column-guided gasholders **138**
   cranes 128
   Crawley **136**
   crown 128, **138**
   frame-guided gasholders 128
   high-pressure bullet tanks **117**, **118**
   high-pressure gasholders 128
   Keyham **138**
   Lavenham 128
   Lymm **138**
   Old Kent Road **131**
   process 128
   resheeting 128
   riveting 98, **106**, 128, **136**, 139
   Saltash **130**
   sheeting installation **135**
   spiral-guided gasholders 128, **134**, **135**, **136**, **137**, **140**, **141**
   support columns 128
   water tanks 128
   waterless gasholders 98, **100**, **106**, **107**, 128
   welded 111, **118**, 128
Cookham, Berkshire **148**
Cornwall
   Falmouth **153**
   Gunnislake **36**
   Helston **74**
   Saltash **130**
corrosion 128
counterweights 15, **16**, **20**, **22**, 35
County Durham, Bishop Auckland **85**
Cowley, Oxfordshire 111, **119**
cranes 128, **130**
Crawley, West Sussex **136**
crown 128, **138**
crown rests 128, **138**
Croydon, London 56, **77**
Cumbria, Grange-over-Sands **147**
Cutler, Samuel 56, **78**, 187, **196**, **197**, **198**
Cutler patent guide frame 187, **196**, **197**, **198**
cylindrical gasholder design 15

Dartford, Kent **78**
Deal, Kent **133**
decorative features 35, **38**, **39**, **40**, **41**, **43**, **52**, **53**

demand 15
design 15
Devon, Torquay **150**
dismantling 144, 165, **206**, **207**, **208**, 218
divers 128, **142**
Dolphinholme, Lancashire 15, **15**, **16**
Dorset
   Bourne Valley, Poole **63**
   Bournemouth **166**
   Isle of Portland **95**
   Poole **122**, **154**
   Sherbourne **7**
   Wareham **96**
   Weymouth **82**

earliest surviving 35
East Greenwich, London 56, 144, **162**, 187, **204**, 205
East Sussex
   Eastbourne **67**
   Hove **26**, 56
Edinburgh, Duke of 165, **171**
environmental legacy 1
Essex
   Canvey Island Liquefied Natural Gas (LNG) Terminal 98, **110**, 111, **112**, **113**, **125**
   Rayleigh **33**, **114**, 144
evolution 15
Exeter, Haven Road **155**

factory lighting 1
Fakenham Gas Museum, Norfolk 1, **8**
Falmouth, Cornwall **153**
Fareham, Hampshire **97**
Farey, Cyril 165, **168**
First World War 165, **178**, **179**
Firth Blakeley 79
flame cleaning **143**
flying lift, the 15, **33**, **76**
four-lift spiral-guided gasholders, Horton Road **84**
frame-guided gasholders **9**, 56, 187
   Aldershot **76**
   Amersham **145**
   Ascot **145**
   Bath **10**, **75**
   Battersea **32**
   Beckton **31**, 56, **57**
   Blackburn **28**, 165
   Bourne Valley, Poole **63**
   bracing 56
   Bradford Road **65**, **66**, **170**, **199**
   construction 128
   Croydon 56, **77**
   Dartford **78**
   East Greenwich 56, **162**, **204**
   Eastbourne **67**

flying lift 33, **76**
Fulham 56, **58**
guide wheels **28**
Helston **74**
Hove **26**, 56
Kennington Oval 56, **60**
Kensal Green 56, **192**, **193**, **194**, **195**
Kingston **92**
lattice shell concept 56
Minehead **149**
New Southgate **70**
Old Kent Road 56, **202**, **203**
Poplar 56, **59**
Rayleigh **33**
Reading **64**
Redheugh **72**, **73**
Southampton **71**
Sydenham 56, **61**
Torquay **150**
Wavertree **68**
Wellingborough **62**
West Ham **69**
Windsor Street **190**, **191**
frameless gasholders 15
Fulham, London 21, 24, 206, **207**, **211**, **212**
 column-guided gasholders 34, 35, **38**, **39**
 frame-guided gasholders 56, **58**
 redevelopment 206, **213**

Gadd and Mason 79
gas companies, first 1
Gas Light and Coke Company (GLCC) 1, 56, 98, 165, **168**, 187
gas production process 1, **5**, 144
gas use 1
gasholder houses 15, **19**, **20**
gasholder stations 79
gasworks 1, 15, 144, 165 *see also* individual sites
Gateshead, Redheugh **72**, **73**
gazomètre, the 15
George III, King 1
girders 35, 56
Gloucester, Horton Road **84**
Gloucestershire, Blakeney 1, **6**
Gordon, Bill 165, **186**
Grange-over-Sands, Cumbria **147**
Great Peter Street, Westminster 1
Great Yarmouth 187, **188**
guide carriages 79, **81**, **85**
guide frames **52**, **53**
guide rails 35, 79
guide wheels 15, **28**, 35, **39**, 144
Gunnislake, Cornwall **36**

Hampshire
 Aldershot **76**
 Basingstoke **130**, **135**
 Fareham **97**
 Southampton **71**
Haven Road, Exeter **155**

Hawksley, Thomas 187, **187**, 189
Helston, Cornwall 74
Hendon, Sunderland 187, **187**
Hertfordshire, Hitchin **14**, 79
high-pressure bullet tanks 15, **33**, 111
 Abingdon **116**, **117**, **118**
 Canvey Island Liquefied Natural Gas (LNG) Terminal **113**
 construction **117**, **118**
 Cowley **119**
 Isle of Grain **120**
 Oakengates **114**
 Rayleigh **114**
 Shanklin **115**
 Skipton **111**, **112**
high-pressure gasholders 111
 Abingdon 111, **116**, **117**, **118**
 Bicester **123**
 Biggin Hill 111, **121**
 Canvey Island Liquefied Natural Gas (LNG) Terminal 111, **112**, **113**, **125**
 Cowley 111, **119**
 Hilsea **124**
 Isle of Grain 111, **120**, **126**
 Oakengates **114**
 pipe array 111, **121**
 Poole **122**
 Rayleigh **114**
 Shanklin **115**
 Skipton 111, **111**, **112**
Hilsea, Portsmouth **124**, 179
Hitchin, Hertfordshire 1, **14**, 79
Hornsey, London **198**
Horton, Horace 111
Horton Road, Gloucester **84**
Hortonspheres 111, **112**, **122**, **123**, **124**
Hove, East Sussex 15, **26**, 56
Huddersfield, Yorkshire **157**
Hunt, Charles 187, **189**, **190**, **191**

impact 1
Imperial GLCC 35
Ipswich, Suffolk 98, **102**
Isle of Grain, Kent 111, **120**, **126**, **127**
Isle of Portland, Dorset **95**
Isle of Wight
 Kingston **92**
 Ryde **30**
 St Helens **88**, **89**
 Shanklin **115**

Jones, Robert and Harry 56

Kennington Oval, London 128, **139**, **185**, **186**
 column-guided gasholders 35, **42**, **43**
 frame-guided gasholders 56, **60**
 redevelopment **218**, **219**, **220**, **221**
Kensal Green, London 56, 187, **192**, **193**, **194**, **195**
Kent
 Dartford **78**

Deal **133**
Isle of Grain 111, **120**, **126**, **127**
Keyham, Plymouth **138**
Kidderminster, Worcestershire **156**
Kings Cross, London 35, **54**, **55**, 165, **173**, **174**, **175**, **208**, **209**, **210**
King's Road Park, London 206
Kingston, Isle of Wight **92**
Klönne, August 98
Klönne gasholders 98
 internal lift **109**
 Ipswich 98
 York 98, **108**
Knapton, William 98

Lancashire
 Blackburn **28**, 165
 Brierfield **146**
 Cloughfold **2**
 Dolphinholme 15, **15**, **16**
lattice shell concept 56
Lavenham, Suffolk 128, **129**
Lavoisier, Antoine 15
legacy 206
Leicester, Aylestone Road **158**
Lincolnshire, Boston **83**
liquefied natural gas (LNG) 98, **110**, 111, **126**, **127**
liquid petroleum gas (LPG) 1, 111, **132–4**
Liverpool
 Bootle 35, **44**, **45**, 128, **140**, **141**
 Wavertree **68**
Livesey, Frank 56, 187
Livesey, George 35, 56, 187, **201**, **202**, **203**
location 144
 rural 144, **144–8**
 transport links 144, **149–55**
 urban 98, **108**, 144, **156–64**
locomotives 1, **12**
London
 Battersea 15, **32**, 98, **99**, **100**, 164, 206, **216**, **217**
 Beckton 1, 4, 6, 12, 15, 31, 35, 40, 56, **57**, **81**, **130**, **137**, **142**, **152**, 165, **168**, **176**, **177**, **180**
 Bethnal Green 15, 27, 56, 144, **163**, 206, **222**, **223**
 Biggin Hill 111, **121**
 Blackfriars 35, **47**
 Bow Common 35, **41**
 Bromley-by-Bow 35, **51**, **52**, **53**, 144, **160**, **161**, 165, **178**, **181**, **182**, **224**, **225**
 Cannon Lane, Pinner **134**
 concentration of gasworks 144
 Croydon 56, **77**
 East Greenwich 144, **162**, **204**
 Fulham 21, 24, 34, 35, **38**, **39**, 56, **58**, 206, 206, **207**, **211**, **212**, **213**
 Hornsey **198**
 Kennington Oval 35, **42**, **43**, 56, **60**, 128, **139**, **185**, **186**, **218**, **219**, **220**, **221**
 Kensal Green 56, **192**, **193**, **194**, **195**
 Kings Cross **54**, **55**, 165, **173**, **174**, **175**, **208**, **209**, **210**
 King's Road Park 206

New Barnet **197**
New Southgate **70**
Old Kent Road 56, **131**, 187, **202**, **203**
Poplar 56, **59**, 144, **160**, 206
Southall 98, **104**
Stanmore 79, **87**
Sydenham 56, **61**
West Ham **69**
Woodford 98, **103**, **132**
Lymm, Cheshire **138**
Lytton Street, Stoke on Trent **172**

maintenance 128, **142**, **143**, 178, 180
MAN gasholders 98
 Battersea 98, **99**, **100**, 164
 Brentford 98
 construction 100, **106**, **107**
 Ipswich **102**
 Kensal Green 98
 Kidderminster **156**
 St Helens **101**
 Southall 98, **104**
 Swan Village 98, **105**, **106**, **107**
 Woodford **103**
Manchester
 Bradford Road **65**, **66**, **139**, 165, **169**, **170**, 187, **199**
 Partington 165, **171**
 Salford **48**
Manchester Corporation 165
Mann, William 35, 47
Maschinenfabrik Augsburg-Nürnberg AG 98
Meadowhall, Sheffield 79, **93**
Merseyside, St Helens **101**
Middlesbrough, Cannon Street **94**
Millbrook, Southampton **29**
Minehead, Somerset **149**
Monkseaton, North Tyneside **3**
Morecambe, White Lund 1, **13**
Murdoch, William x, 1, **18**

National Gas Museum **158**
natural gas network 111
Neepsend, Sheffield 33, **91**, **92**
New Barnet, London **197**
New Southgate, London **70**
Newbigging, John 187
Newbigging, Thomas 187, **201**
Newton Chambers 79
Norfolk, Fakenham Gas Museum 1, **8**
North Sea natural gas 111
North Tyneside, Willington Quay **90**
Northampton **12**
Northamptonshire, Wellingborough **62**
Northwich, Cheshire 79
Norwich, Bishop Bridge Road **86**
number scale 79, **96**

Oakengates, Shropshire **109**, **114**
obsolescence 206
offices 144

Old Kent Road, London 56, **131**, 187, **202**, **203**
operation 1
Oval Cricket Ground 165, **185**, **186**
Oxford 20
Oxfordshire
    Abingdon 111, **116**, **117**, **118**
    Bicester **123**
    Cowley 111, **119**

Paddon, John 15, **26**, 56
painting 128, **141**, **143**, **178**, **180**
Partington, Manchester 165, **171**
patch welding 128, **142**
Philips and Lee 1
Pickering, Yorkshire **143**
pistons 98, **107**
Plymouth, Keyham **138**
Poole, Dorset **122**, **154**
Poplar, London 56, **59**, 144, **160**, 206
Portsmouth 35, **50**
    Hilsea **124**, **179**
Practical Treatise on Gas Light (Accum) 15, **17**
Preston, Lancashire 35, **37**
promotional material 165, **196**, **200**

R&J Dempster **80**
Rayleigh, Essex **33**, **114**, 144
Reading, Berkshire **64**, **159**
recreation grounds 165, **183**
redevelopment 35, 165, 206
    Battersea 206, **217**
    Bethnal Green 206, **223**
    Canon's Marsh **215**
    Fulham 206, **213**
    Kennington Oval **218**, **220**, **221**
    Kings Cross **175**, **209**, **210**
    Poplar 206
Redheugh, Gateshead **72**, **73**
resheeting 128, **143**
retort houses **4**
riveting 98, 128, **139**
rolled steel joists (RSJ) 56
Rossendale Union Gas Company **2**, 187
rotary scrubbers **6**
rotating gasholder design 15
Royal Society 15
rural locations 144, **144–8**
Ryde, Isle of Wight 15, **30**

safety concerns 15
St Helens, Isle of Wight **88**, **89**
St Helens, Merseyside **101**
Salford, Manchester 1, 35, **48**
Saltash, Cornwall **130**
Saltisford, Warwick **19**
Samuel Cutler and Sons 187
Scarborough, Yorkshire 35, **46**
Scotch derricks **134**
scrubbers **6**, **7**
Second World War **150**, 165, **176**, **177**, **180**

Shanklin, Isle of Wight **115**
Sheffield
    Meadowhall 79, **93**
    Neepsend **33**, **91**, **92**
Sherbourne, Dorset 1, **7**
Shropshire, Oakengates **109**, **113**
significance 206
single-lift column-guided gasholders **34**
single-lift gasholders **22**
sites 144
size limits 35
Skipton, Yorkshire 111, **111**, **112**
Smethwick, West Midlands **18**
social role 165
Somerset, Minehead **149**
South Metropolitan Gas Company 56, 187
South Shields, Tyne and Wear **25**
Southall, London **104**
Southampton, Hampshire **71**
    Millbrook **29**
Southern Gas Board **166**, **183**
Sowerby Bridge, Willow Hall Mill 1
Spice, Robert Paulson 187, **188**, **189**
spiral-guided gasholders 15, 79, **80**
    Ascot **145**
    Basingstoke **135**
    Battersea **32**
    Beckton **6**, **31**, **81**, **137**
    Birkshall **94**
    Bishop Auckland **85**
    Bishop Bridge Road **86**
    Bootle **140**, **141**
    Boston **83**
    Cannon Lane, Pinner **134**
    colour scheme 79, **87**
    construction 128, **134**, **135**, **136**, **137**, **140**, **141**
    Crawley **136**
    Fareham **97**
    four-lift **84**
    Grange-over-Sands **147**
    guide carriage 79, **81**, **85**
    guide rails 79
    Hitchin **79**
    Horton Road **84**
    Isle of Portland **95**
    Kingston **92**
    lifts 79
    Lytton Street **172**
    Meadowhall 79, **93**
    Middlesbrough **94**
    Millbrook **29**
    Neepsend **91**, **92**
    Northwich 79
    Rayleigh **33**
    Ryde **30**
    St Helens **88**, **89**
    Stanmore 79, **87**
    three-lift **29**, 79, **82**, **83**, **95**
    two-lift 79, **88**, **89**, **147**
    visibility 79, **82**, **83**, **84**, **85**, **86**

Wareham **96**
Weymouth **82**
Willington Quay **90**
sports clubs 165, 183, **184**, **185**, **186**
staff 165, **166**
Staffordshire, Stone 165, **167**
standards 56, **74**
Stanmore, London 79, **87**
Stapleton Road, Bristol **184**
steel 15, 56, 79, **91**, **94**, **95**, 98, 111, 128, **130**, 144, **145**
Stoke on Trent, Lytton Street **172**
Stone, Staffordshire 165, **167**
street lighting 1, **3**
Suffolk
    Ipswich 98, **102**
    Lavenham 128, **129**
Sunderland, Hendon 187, **187**
Sunderland Gas Company 187
supply storage 1
support columns 15, 56
    cast iron 35, **40**
    conjoined 128, **139**
    construction 128
    decorative features 35, **38**, **39**, **40**, **41**, **43**
    guide wheels 35
    square 35
    tripod 15, **21**, **24**, **34**, 35
Surrey, Ascot **145**
Swan Village, West Bromwich 98, **105**, **106**, **107**
Sydenham, London 56, **61**

telescopic gasholder design 15, **23**
telescopic lifts **9**
tent-shaped gasholder design 15
three-lift column-guided gasholders 35, **47**
three-lift spiral-guided gasholders
    Boston **83**
    Hitchin **79**
    Isle of Portland **95**
    Weymouth **82**
ties 35, 56
Torquay, Devon **150**
transport links 1, 144, **149–55**, 165, **172**, **173**, **174**
Trewby, George 15, **27**, 56, 187
tripod-guided gasholders **34**, 35
Tunbridge Wells 187
two-lift column-guided gasholders 35, **44**, **45**, **46**, **143**
two-lift spiral-guided gasholders 79
    Grange-over-Sands **147**
    St Helens **88**, **89**
Tyne and Wear, South Shields **25**

urban locations 98, **108**, 144, **156–64**

Wareham, Dorset **96**
Warwick, Saltisford **19**
washers **6**, **7**
water seals **9**
water tanks 15, 128
waterless gasholders 98

Battersea **32**, 98, **99**, **100**, **164**
Brentford 98
Canvey Island Liquefied Natural Gas (LNG) Terminal 98, **110**
construction 128
Ipswich 98, **102**
Kensal Green 98
Kidderminster **156**
Oakengates **109**
pistons 98
St Helens **101**
Southall 98, **104**
Swan Village 98, **105**, **106**, **107**
Woodford **103**
York 98, **108**
waterproofing 128
Wavertree, Liverpool **68**
Wellingborough, Northamptonshire **62**
West Bromwich, Swan Village 98, **105**, **106**, **107**
West Ham, London **69**
West Midlands, Smethwick **18**
West Sussex, Crawley **136**
Westminster, Great Peter Street 1
Westwood & Wright 35
Weymouth, Dorset **82**
Whitby, Yorkshire **151**
White Lund, Morecambe 1, **13**
Wiggins gasholders 98, **109**, **110**
Willington Quay, North Tyneside **90**
Willow Hall Mill, Sowerby Bridge 1
wind ties 56
Windsor, Berkshire 1, **11**
Windsor Street, Birmingham 187, **190**, **191**
Winzer, Friedrich 1, **2**
wire-rope-guided gasholders 15
Woodall, Corbett 56
Woodford, London **103**, **132**
Worcestershire, Kidderminster **156**
wrought iron 15, 56
Wyatt, Vitruvius 56, 187

York 98, **108**, 159
Yorkshire
    Castleford **143**
    Huddersfield **157**
    Scarborough **46**
    Skipton 111, **111**
    Whitby **151**